W9-AAD-933

FINGERPRINTS

For Doug, one of the "1817 Oak Street Boys,"
who always kept the rest of us on track—and accountable!

Acknowledgments

This book would not have become a reality without the loving support of my wife, Joan. In addition, she and my daughter, Caroline, graciously contributed to many of the illustrations in this book. Thanks to Joe Elliot and Mathew Bacon of School Specialty for their support. Special thanks to Ken Rando for helping me with the electrons. Thank you to Lawrence Quarino, Ph.D., D-ABC, Director of Forensic Science Program, Cedar Crest College, Allentown, PA, for his careful reading of the manuscript and many helpful comments and suggestions.

Library of Congress Cataloging-in-Publication Data

Rainis, Kenneth G.
  Fingerprints : crime-solving science experiments / Kenneth G. Rainis.
    p. cm. — (Forensic science projects)
  Includes bibliographical references and index.
  ISBN 0-7660-1960-8
    1. Fingerprints—Juvenile literature. 2. Criminal investigation—
  Juvenile literature. I. Title.
  HV6074.R26 2006
  363.25'8—dc22
                                                      2005036760

Printed in the United States of America

10 9 8 7 6 5 4 3 2 1

To Our Readers: We have done our best to make sure all Internet Addresses in this book were active and appropriate when we went to press. However, the author and the publisher have no control over and assume no liability for the material available on those Internet sites or on other Web sites they may link to. Any comments or suggestions can be sent by e-mail to comments@enslow.com or to the address on the back cover.

Every effort has been made to locate all copyright holders of material used in this book. If any errors or omissions have occurred, corrections will be made in future editions of this book.

Illustration Credits: All illustrations by Kenneth G. Rainis, except as follows: © 2006 by Stephen Rountree (www.rountreegraphics.com), pp. 30, 43, 83, 98; © 2006 Jupiterimages Corporation, pp. 56, 95; Arresting Images p. 10; Biophoto Associates / Photo Researchers, Inc., p. 20; Federal Bureau of Investigation, pp. 9, 89; James King-Holmes / Photo Researchers, Inc., p. 61; Justice Denied Magazine, Issue 25, Summer 2004, p. 73 (a, b), 115 (b); NeoSCI, a division of Delta Education LLC, Nashua, New Hampshire, a School Specialty Science company, pp. 19, 25, 108; Mauro Fermariello / Photo Researchers, Inc., p. 7; Michael Donne / Photo Researchers, Inc., p. 38; Shutterstock.com, p. 28 (b).

Background Illustration Credits: Biophoto Associates / Photo Researchers, Inc. (hand print); Kenneth G. Rainis (fingerprint clip art); Phanie / Photo Researchers, Inc. (chapter openers).

Cover Photo: © 2006 Jupiterimages Corporation.

FINGERPRINTS

Crime-Solving
Science
Experiments

Kenneth G. Rainis

Science Consultant:

Brian Gestring, M.S.
Director of Forensic Science Program
Pace University
New York, New York

Enslow Publishers, Inc.
40 Industrial Road
Box 398
Berkeley Heights, NJ 07922
USA

http://www.enslow.com

CONTENTS

The Case of the Silent Witness

On Monday, March 28, 1994, Ann Ferguson was running late. She had a meeting with her friend, Rose Connor. She arrived at Connor's Florida estate thinking that Rose would be annoyed. She went to the door, opened it, and entered the house. She called Rose's name. There was no reply. Ann went searching for her friend. She found her, dead, lying facedown on her bed. Ferguson ran to the kitchen to telephone the police.

Orange County Sheriff's deputies followed standard procedure and began interviewing neighbors. Maybe someone had heard or seen something. The house painter next door said that he had heard a woman's screams coming from the Connor house between 9:30 and 10:30 A.M. the previous morning. The neighbor remembered seeing a man with black hair around the house that morning.

Crime scene technicians fingerprinted Ann Ferguson and the deceased. These were "elimination prints"—they would help eliminate their fingerprints from other evidence. They also collected latent (not visible) fingerprints in the master bedroom by using a white powder to see them on dark surfaces, then special sticky tape to lift

When a suspect is fingerprinted,
the finger is rolled in ink.
Then the print can be transferred
to a fingerprint card. Each
person's fingerprints are unique.

them from the surface of the bedpost. They used a black powder to reveal fingerprints found on the white tiles in the bathroom shower stall. The deputies applied a chemical called ninhydrin to the walls of the hallway, master bedroom door, and bathroom. A deputy photographed a purse that was found open and took it as evidence. After close inspection, deputies noticed that the purse contained no credit cards or bankcards.

Two days later, deputies returned to the house to gather more evidence. They photographed the purplish-colored latent prints exposed by the ninhydrin on the walls and door frame. They used a white powder to expose latent fingerprints on a glass left on the kitchen counter. Deputies opened the bathroom drains and recovered hair samples. The victim had a boyfriend who was an overnight visitor in her home; therefore, one would expect his hair to be found at the scene. They took known hair samples from the boyfriend to later compare with recovered hair samples.

Deputies began looking into Rose Connor's credit card transactions. They also reviewed videotapes from local bank automatic teller machines (ATMs). The camera of an ATM at a bank in Longwood, Florida, gave deputies a link to Rose Connor's stolen bankcard account number—and a possible suspect. The person was fifty-two-year old Kenneth Eldon Lott.

Lott had numerous previous convictions for armed robbery and grand theft, and had served time in prison.

Lott told authorities that he knew the victim and used to work for her doing landscaping. He had an alibi. He had been at his mother's house all day on Sunday, March 27. He told authorities he had not been inside the Connor house. However, Lott admitted to using Connor's ATM card and the PIN number.

On April 21, a deputy went to Ken Lott's home in Deltona, Florida, and took a V-necked shirt into evidence, placing it in a sealed paper evidence bag.

Meanwhile a fingerprint analyst at the sheriff's office began entering the collected

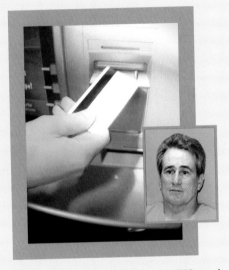

Kenneth Lott used Connor's ATM card.

fingerprint evidence into AFIS—the Automated Fingerprint Identification System set up by the Federal Bureau of Investigation (FBI) in 1997. The analyst electronically scanned each fingerprint into the national database. The database returned a list of possible matches. A fingerprint examiner inspected these possible matches.

In her pretrial report, the analyst stated that four latent fingerprints found in the house were identified as the suspect's. One print was found on the left door jam of the master bedroom. Two prints were found on the exterior glass of the front door, and on the front edge of

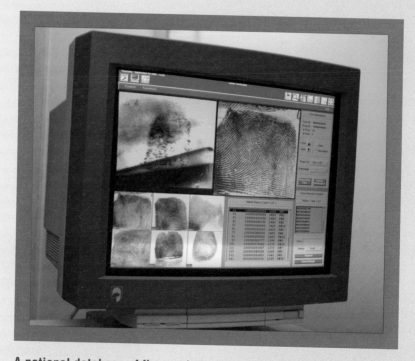

A national database of fingerprints allows comparison of fingerprints from a crime scene with prints in the database.

a sink in the master bedroom. The fourth print, a thumbprint, was found on the bedpost.

At the trace evidence section of the forensic lab, an analyst began examining hair and fiber evidence. Hairs collected in the bathroom sink and on the bed were compared under a microscope to hair from the suspect, the victim, the victim's boyfriend, and Ann Ferguson. Ken Lott has graying black hair. Both Rose Connor and Ann Ferguson had brown hair that had been colored. The boyfriend had blonde hair. The analyst identified black hairs recovered from the bathroom sink and on Connor's body.

The analyst also examined recovered wool fibers from the master bedroom carpet. She then compared these fibers under the microscope to those recovered from the suspect's T-shirt. Her pretrial report stated that the recovered T-shirt fibers were "consistent" with the wool carpet fibers.

The forensic lab presented the trace evidence and its analysis in a pretrial report to the Orange County district attorney. Its findings all pointed to Kenneth Lott. On May 20, 1994, the grand jury sent Ken Lott to trial.

At trial, the fingerprint and trace fiber evidence placed Lott inside the Connor home. The prosecution argued that Lott and an accomplice had intended to rob Connor because they needed drug money. Both were high on drugs at the time of attempted robbery. The robbery did not go as planned. Lott killed Connor because she could identify him. A jury found Lott guilty of first-degree murder. On June 23, 1995, Kenneth Eldon Lott was sentenced to die for the murder of Rose Connor.

Physical Evidence

Every crime leaves a visible sign, a "silent witness" called physical evidence. Physical evidence can lead a careful investigator back to the perpetrator—the individual who committed the crime. Fingerprints are one type of physical evidence.

Fingerprinting is an old science. It was used by the ancient Chinese, who recorded it in drawings on official wax seals attached to important state documents. Fingerprints and toe prints are known as friction ridge patterns. These tiny ridges in the outer skin develop before birth. Friction ridge patterns are also present on palms and pads of feet. The arrangement and number of these friction ridges are unique to every individual. It is this uniqueness that allows analysts to identify, describe, and compare these patterns to help solve a crime.

Tools You Will Need

You will use this book as a guide in learning how to analyze fingerprints. In the process, you will see how fingerprint analysis is used to solve crimes and various mysteries.

All forensic investigators carry a case notebook. You should too. It will help you to collect facts about the cases you are working on and record and organize data.

Every crime leaves a visible sign, a "silent witness" called *physical evidence.*

For most fingerprint analyses, you will not need any "high-tech" materials. Some techniques will require special chemicals that can be obtained through your local science teacher. (There are "inkless" cards for use in fingerprinting; see Appendix for sources.)

Forensic Examination and the Scientific Method

Fingerprint investigators used an important procedure—the scientific method—to match recovered evidence to Ken Lott and conclusively link him to the murder of Rose Connor. They followed these steps in their analyses: They observed the fingerprint data. They made a careful guess (a theory) to explain what was observed. They designed or used a method (an experiment) to test their guess and come up with a hypothesis (a tested theory). They then used the results (data) to conclude whether their guess was correct or whether it should be changed. All forensic scientists use the scientific method to focus their investigation on significant evidence and to come to conclusions.

All forensic scientists must summarize and report their findings (conclusions) to law enforcement authorities and the court. They present formal pretrial reports and verbal testimony. At times you will be asked to prepare a report for the Court. Your pretrial report should contain the following parts and be in this order:

- Observation of data
- Interpretation of data
- Hypothesis
- Testing of hypothesis and procedures followed
- Summary; findings of fact

Your pretrial report should be word processed, typed, or written clearly in blue or black ink. It can also include the following:

- The importance of the finding in relation to the events of the case.
- The strengths and limitations of the evidence.

Keeping Safe as a Junior Fingerprint Examiner

The most important ingredient for success is safety.

1. Be serious about forensic science. An easygoing attitude can be dangerous to you and to others. Always investigate under the supervision of a knowledgeable adult.

2. Read instructions carefully and completely before beginning with any case in this book. Discuss your investigative procedure with a knowledgeable adult before you start. A flaw in your design could cause an accident. If in doubt, check with a science teacher or other knowledgeable adult.

3. Keep your work area clean and organized. Never eat or drink anything while conducting investigations.

4. Wear safety glasses when working with chemicals or when performing any other experiment that could lead to eye injury.

5. Do not touch chemicals with your bare hands unless instructed to do so. Do not taste chemicals or chemical solutions. Do not inhale vapors or fumes from any chemical or chemical solution.

6. Clean up any chemical spill immediately. If you spill anything on your skin or clothing, rinse it off immediately with plenty of water. Then report what happened to a responsible adult.

7. Keep flammable liquids away from heat sources.

8. Always wash your hands after conducting experiments. Dispose of contaminated waste or articles properly.

9. Be a responsible "Web surfer"—explore only genuine topic areas approved by a responsible adult.

How This Book Is Organized

Chapter 1 of this book gave you a true-life example of how an individual left behind physical signs of his presence at a crime scene. Fingerprint analysis was then used to link the perpetrator to the crime scene. Chapter 2 gives you important background information about fingerprints—how they can be collected and analyzed to identify an individual or place an individual at the crime scene. You will learn how fingerprint analysts do their work.

In Chapter 3, you can read about actual cases that are solved by examining fingerprint evidence. Each of these cases has a project that will provide you with more forensic skills. It also has some science project ideas to practice and expand on what you have learned. You may decide to use one of these ideas as a start to your own science fair project.

In Chapter 4, you and your friends will have an opportunity to use your newly acquired analysis skills to solve a mock crime that closely follows true events. Like all professional forensic analysts, you will need to write a report that provides a clear conclusion from your analysis results.

Lastly, you can go to Chapter 5 to get explanations to the various questions and cases contained in this book. Let's get to work!

CHAPTER 2

Fingerprint Analysis

The first scientific recognition of fingerprints happened in the seventeenth century. Two hundred years later, in 1892, Sir Francis Galton published a book, *Finger Prints*, in which he proposed that no two fingers have identical friction ridge characteristics and that fingerprints remain unchanged during a person's lifetime. Today, law enforcement officials use fingerprints to identify people.

Types of Fingerprint Evidence

There are three main types of fingerprint evidence. The first is the plastic (indented) fingermark. This is a three-dimensional fingertip impression in a soft substance, such as wax, putty, or drying paint. The second type is the patent (visible) fingermark. This is like a bloody fingerprint left on a clear drinking glass. You can see it. The third and most common type of fingerprint evidence is the latent (invisible) fingermark. This type of print also causes the most problems. These prints are largely invisible, and generally require some form of physical or chemical treatment to make them visible.

But what are fingerprints, exactly?

Fingerprints Are Friction Ridges

The palms of your hands and the soles of your feet have a series of raised patterns called friction ridges. Friction ridges are formed before birth. The number, shape, and relative location of these ridges make each person's prints unique. Each friction ridge has a single row of pores that are openings for sweat glands. Perspiration comes out of these pores to the skin's surface. Once a finger touches a surface, perspiration and body oils (from touching your face or hair) are transferred to that surface in the form of an impression of the friction ridge pattern. A fingerprint is the result (see Figure 1).

In 1924, the FBI Identification Division was created. Currently, the FBI has over 250 million sets of fingerprint records. This enormous collection is made up of both criminal and civil prints. Individuals who

There are three main types of fingerprint evidence: *plastic, visible, and latent.*

FIGURE 1
●●●●●●●●●●●●●●●●●

You and Your Fingerprint

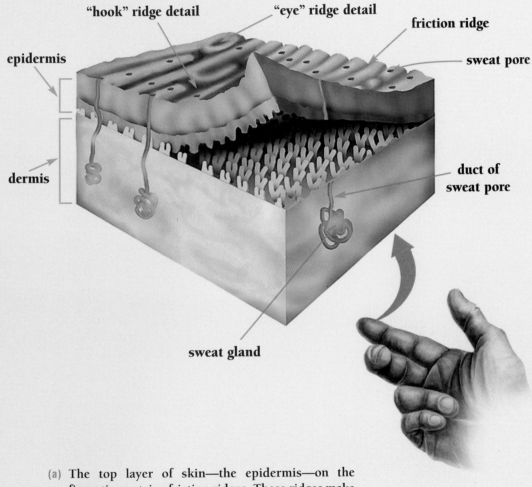

"hook" ridge detail   "eye" ridge detail   friction ridge

epidermis   sweat pore

dermis   duct of sweat pore

sweat gland

(a) The top layer of skin—the epidermis—on the fingertip contains friction ridges. These ridges make a fingerprint unique. When the finger touches a surface, perspiration and oils are transferred to that surface in the form of an impression of the friction ridge pattern. A fingerprint is formed.

●●●●●●●●●●●●●●●●●●

This photo of a human fingertip shows the raised friction ridges.

have been arrested and/or convicted of a crime are included in the criminal collection. The civil file includes the prints of both government employees and applicants for federal jobs.

The FBI has developed a system called AFIS, which stands for Automated Fingerprint Identification System. This system provides national fingerprint checks without the use of fingerprint cards. When police officers take suspects' prints digitally, on an electronic pad, the prints can be stored in the AFIS database. The database can compare prints almost immediately with millions of digitized prints on file in the FBI computer banks and suggest possible matches.

Increasingly, security access systems, such as doors that require a code or password to enter, utilize fingerprints. In these systems, a laser scans the ridge patterns of individuals who must press their fingers against a plate. This digital scan is then compared with stored data of security-cleared personnel. A match allows entry.

Fingerprint ridge patterns may be grouped into three large categories: the arch, the loop, and the whorl. In the arch pattern, the friction ridges extend across the bulb of the finger and rise slightly at the center. The loop pattern consists of one or more ridges curving into a hairpin turn. Ridges in the whorl pattern create a spiral or circle on the finger. These main groupings can be further divided into eight distinct patterns used for identification purposes, as shown in Table 1.

TABLE 1. Ridge Patterns of Central Area of Fingerprint

ARCH	LOOP	WHORL
Ridgelines start from one side of the fingertip, rise at the center, and exit on the other side of the fingertip.	Ridgelines start and end on the same side of the fingertip.	Ridgelines are circles that do not begin or end on either side of the fingertip.
Plain Arch 	Radial Loop 	Plain Whorl
Tented Arch 	Ulnar Loop 	Central Pocket Loop
		Double Loop
		Accidental Whorl

There are three fundamental principles of fingerprints:

1. Fingerprints have general fingerprint ridge patterns (arch, loop, and whorl) that allow for classification.
2. A fingerprint is an individual characteristic. No two fingers have yet been found to have identical friction ridge patterns.
3. Fingerprints will remain unchanged during an individual's lifetime.

You have now learned that a fingerprint is a unique physical characteristic that can be used to identify a particular individual within a group or population. Scientists call this individualization—the ability to identify a specific individual using a distinguishing feature. Many people have an arch ridge pattern, but no two people with an arch ridge pattern have an exact matching set of identical ridgeline patterns. Forensic science is about excluding individuals from a population of possible suspects.

You will now learn how to recover and analyze fingerprints to eliminate or include a person from consideration in a forensic case. Later, you will use these same detection skills to investigate similar cases of your own.

PROJECT:
Practicing Fingerprint Ridge Identification Skills

What You Need:

- photocopy of Figure 2
- access to a photocopier
- magnifying glass (10–20X)
- pen or pencil

What You Do:

1. Make a photocopy of the fingerprint in Figure 2.
2. Use a magnifying glass to examine the photocopied fingerprint.
3. Use Table 1 to help you determine what fingerprint pattern (e.g. arch, loop, or whorl) the fingerprint is. Write down your classification underneath the fingerprint.
4. Try to identify separate fingerprint ridge details (see Table 2). How many of the ten ridge types can you find? Circle the ridge detail on your copy of the print. Draw a line from the circle and label the line with the ridge detail name.

FIGURE 2

Practice Fingerprint

Make a photocopy of this fingerprint. Then examine it with a magnifying glass. What fingerprint pattern do you observe? How many different ridgeline details can you identify?

Which fingerprint ridge detail is most common in this fingerprint? The rarest? Check your results with the author's analysis in Chapter 5.

TABLE 2. Fingerprint Ridgeline Details

Ending Ridge	
Fork	
Short Ridge	
Dot	
Bridge	
Hook	
Eye	
Double Fork	
Delta	
Triple Fork	

PROJECT:

Making a "Ten-print" Fingerprint File

A direct print is a known fingerprint made from an individual. Fingerprint examiners regularly refer to the paper card that holds all ten direct fingerprints as a "ten-print file." Let's make a set of ten direct fingerprints of a friend and begin to create a fingerprint database.

What You Need:

- ruler
- pen
- fingerprint card blank (Figure 3)
- index cards (5 x 8 inches)
- a friend
- No. 2 pencil
- pencil sharpener
- ¾-inch transparent sticky tape in tape dispenser
- scissors
- magnifying glass (10–20X)
- access to a photocopier

What You Do:

1. Use a ruler and a pen to copy the design and text of the fingerprint card (Figure 3) onto a 5 x 8-inch index card.
2. Ask a friend's permission to allow you to fingerprint him or her.
3. Sharpen a No. 2 (soft) pencil using a pencil sharpener.

27

FIGURE 3

Fingerprint Card

(a)

RIGHT HAND

1 Thumb	2 Index Finger	3 Middle Finger	4 Ring Finger	5 Little Finger

LEFT HAND

6 Thumb	7 Index Finger	8 Middle Finger	9 Ring Finger	10 Little Finger

(b)

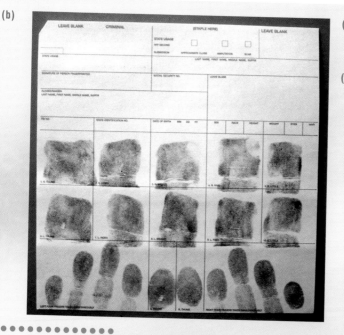

(a) This blank fingerprint card is based upon the FBI model.

(b) A 10-print sample shows two types of impressions— 10 rolled impressions (top two rows), and a bottom set of "slabbed" or "flat" impressions that are used to verify the sequence and accuracy of the rolled impressions.

4. Rub a No. 2 pencil on your friend's right-hand little finger fingertip. Make sure that the entire tip area is covered (see Figure 4a).

5. Carefully grasp the *edge* of the transparent tape in its dispenser and pull it outward *about an inch*. Do not tear off the tape. Do NOT touch the bottom of the tape that has been unrolled (see Figure 4b).

6. Have your friend extend the graphite-coated right-hand little finger toward you.

7. Position the untouched portion of the extended tape above the right little finger. Carefully press the tape down onto the extended fingertip so that the graphite fingerprint will stick to the tape (see Figure 4c).

8. Use a steady upward motion to gently pull the tape up off the fingertip.

9. Carefully tear off the piece of tape.

10. Position the captured right little finger fingerprint over the box labeled "R LITTLE" on the 5 x 8-inch index card.

11. Carefully press the tape, containing the fingerprint, onto the paper (see Figure 4d). Trim any excess tape with scissors.

12. Repeat the print-lifting process with the right ring, middle, index, and thumb fingers.

13. Repeat Steps 4 through 12 with the fingertips of the left hand.

14. At the top of the fingerprint card, record: the individual's name, date of birth, gender, eye color, place of birth, and height.

FIGURE 4

Making a Direct Impression Fingerprint

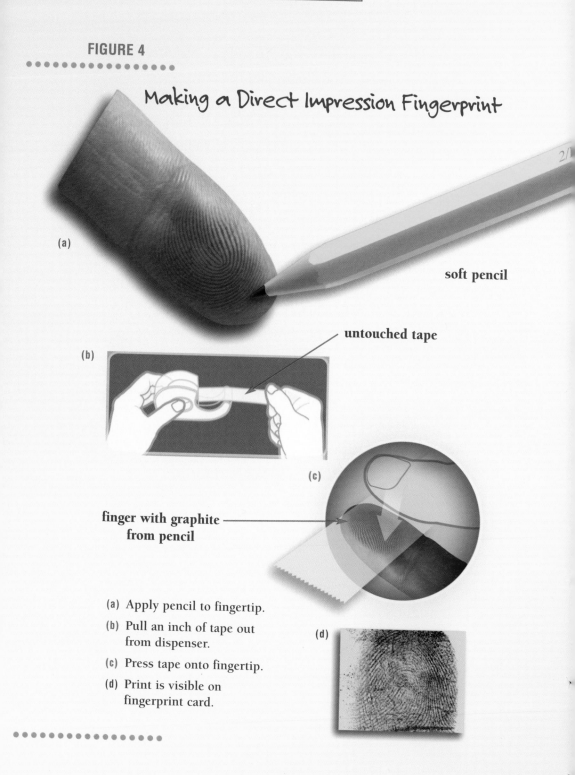

(a)

soft pencil

untouched tape

(b)

(c)

finger with graphite
from pencil

(a) Apply pencil to fingertip.

(b) Pull an inch of tape out
from dispenser.

(c) Press tape onto fingertip.

(d) Print is visible on
fingerprint card.

(d)

15. Use a 10–20X magnifying glass to carefully examine each of the ten prints on the fingerprint card. Using Table 1 as a guide, record the abbreviation for one of the eight fingerprint patterns at the *bottom left* of each finger square: "PA" (plain arch); "TA" (tented arch), "RL" (radial loop), "UL" (ulnar loop), "PW" (plain whorl), "CL" (central pocket loop), "DL" (double loop), and "AW" (accidental whorl).

16. Use a photocopier to make copies of this original record for your analysis investigations. Use the "contrast" button on the machine to make dark, clear copies.

Science Project Idea

Can you use an inkpad instead of a pencil to create fingerprints? Which prints are clearer and easier to analyze? Is there an amount of ink that is too much, making the prints unclear?

Steps in Analyzing and Comparing Fingerprints

Comparison of fingerprints for purposes of identification focuses on three different levels of details:

Level I detail focuses on identifying the general type of the central area of the fingerprint, such as an arch, whorl, or loop.

Level II detail focuses on the unique patterns of ridge paths, such as places where ridges split or end or create dots or islands. These features provide a great deal of detail. Level II detail can be used to identify one individual finger from among the entire human population as the source of a latent print.

Level III detail focuses on tiny features such as pores on a ridge and the width and shape of the ridge itself and its edges.

A fingerprint examiner goes through a four-step process called "ACE-V," for *a*nalysis, *c*omparison, *e*valuation, and *v*erification. At the first stage, *analysis*, the examiner studies the latent print from the crime scene and identifies the key features at levels I, II, and (if possible) III that can be used for identification purposes. The examiner then looks at a known print (an electronic image from a database or an actual print from a fingerprint card) and analyzes it for key features. At the second stage, *comparison*, the examiner simply compares the latent print and the known print, feature by feature, to see if they match. During *evaluation*, the examiner decides if there is (a) a match, (b) no match, or (c) not enough information to decide. Lastly, a second examiner *verifies* the results.

Tips For
Analyzing Fingerprints

1. Analyze only photocopies; keep the original records safe.
2. Use a 10–20X magnifying glass to examine a fingerprint.
3. Determine which fingerprint patterns the print has.
4. Always compare prints having the same fingerprint ridge pattern (loop, arch, or whorl).
5. Use a photocopier to identically enlarge each print for comparison, or use a magnifying glass.
6. Use scissors to cut out each print. Use a glue stick to glue them on a clean sheet of white paper so that they are *oriented in the same way*.
7. Use a 10–20X magnifying glass to carefully scan a like area of each fingerprint(s) for matching fingerprint ridgeline details. Use Table 2 as a guide.
8. Mastering the specifics of fingerprint identification or comparison takes careful study. When experts compare two fingerprints, they usually require twelve to fifteen points of similarity between the two to establish that the prints are identical; that is, from the same individual.

P R O J E C T :

Practicing Your Fingerprint Analysis Skills

What You Need:

- Figure 5
- access to a photocopier
- magnifying glass, 10–20X
- pen or pencil
- ruler
- fingerprint card blank (Figure 3a)
- index cards (5 x 8 inches)
- as many people as you can find who are willing to give you fingerprint samples, including identical twins
- No. 2 pencil
- pencil sharpener
- ¾-inch transparent sticky tape in tape dispenser
- scissors

What You Do:

1. Make a photocopy of Figure 5. Use a magnifying glass to compare each of the three prints. On the photocopy, record the fingerprint pattern and circle points of similarity. Compare your analysis to the author's in Chapter 5.

2. If possible, take one hundred or more fingerprints from as many people as you can. Examine each of the prints using a magnifying glass. Classify each fingerprint by general type (arch, loop, whorl). In your notebook, keep track of which type appears on each finger for each individual you examine. If possible, include identical twins in your survey. After your analysis, answer these questions:

What general type (loop, arch, whorl) is most common? What general type is most uncommon? Can an individual have more than one general type fingerprint? Do identical twins have the same fingerprint type; on each finger? See Chapter 5 for an analysis.

FIGURE 5

Comparison of Three Fingerprints

Compare these three prints, using a magnifying glass. What fingerprint pattern do they have? Do you find points of similarity?

CHAPTER 3

Inspector's Casebook

The cases in this chapter are actual cases involving the use of fingerprint evidence that helped convict individuals. You will learn how forensic fingerprint examiners solved these cases. Then you will use these same detection skills to solve similar cases of your own.

CASE #1

The Case of the Solitary Fingerprint

OBJECTIVE: To detect latent fingerprints on smooth surfaces.

THE SCOUNDREL: David Jeffrey Meyer (1959–   )

THE CRIME: FIRST-DEGREE MURDER. On the afternoon of Monday, March 8, 2004, sixty-six-year-old attorney Fred Parker knew his life was ebbing away. He had been stabbed eleven times in a public restroom in a Florida mall. His only thought was to reach the nearby restaurant and call for help. He collapsed as he stepped inside the restaurant's entrance. Frightened staff

36

immediately called 9–1–1. Emergency medical technicians arrived too late for Fred Parker. He was pronounced dead at the scene.

The Tallahassee Police Department (TPD) had arrived with the ambulance. The officers asked that the Homicide-Assault Unit be notified. Unit officers classified Parker's death a homicide—the unlawful killing of a person.

The TPD forensics unit was called to process the crime scene—the place where Parker lay. They followed a trail of blood back to the restroom. Forensic specialist Jeff Fennell spent five hours trying to find any hidden (latent) fingerprints that might have been left by the murderer. He knew that fingerprints are impressions caused by perspiration and oils on the ridges of the skin that makes the print mark. He also knew that these print marks were mostly water—along with traces of salt, amino acids (the building blocks of proteins), and perhaps oil, dirt, grease, or blood. His job was to use materials that would combine with the latent print and make it visible.

He began by using white and black powders. The tile in the restroom was gray, so he began by using a black graphite powder. He could have also used a white powder. He applied a very thin coating of black powder using a fluffy dusting brush. If any latent fingerprints were left behind, the particles of graphite would cling to the ridge marks and produce a visible fingerprint.

Fennell and other investigators also took a number of "elimination prints"—inked (direct) fingerprints from restaurant workers and other individuals to help eliminate fingerprint matches found at the crime scene.

Fennell's dusting yielded a number of visible prints. He used wide sticky tape to carefully lift each print and preserve it by placing the tape onto a white evidence card. Later, these recovered prints were scanned by a

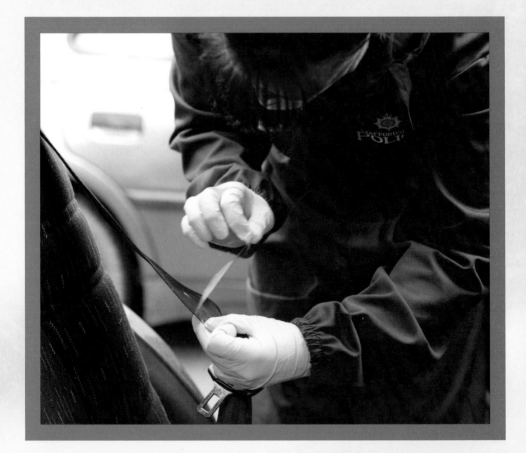

Crime officers use tape to lift fingerprints from a crime scene. Officers wear gloves so they do not contaminate the evidence.

computer in the Leon County Sheriff's Office and entered into the national AFIS database maintained by the FBI. A number of possible matches came back.

Fingerprint examiners went to work reviewing each preliminary match. Only a single fingerprint provided new clues. It was obtained from the Palm Beach County Sheriff's Office and linked to a suspect in another, similar homicide. The TPD investigators developed enough probable cause (sufficient reason to arrest or search a suspect) to suspect David Jeffrey Meyer. Meyer was a drifter, known to be living at a motel close to the murder scene.

Early on the morning of Thursday, March 11, police arrested Meyer at his motel, after a brief chase in the outside motel corridor. He was handcuffed and led away. They then obtained a search warrant to search his motel room. The search yielded additional physical evidence. Meyer was charged with first-degree murder.

After trial, on August 4, 2005, Meyer was found guilty of the first-degree murder of Fred Parker. On August 12, he was sentenced to life imprisonment without parole.

When interviewed by reporter James Rosica of the *Tallahassee Democrat*, forensic specialist Fennell said, "People lie. Physical evidence doesn't lie."

PROJECT:

Dusting for Latent Fingerprints

See if you can find and image a latent fingerprint, recover it, and identify its source.

What You Need:

- pen
- 3 index cards (4 x 5 inches)
- 2 friends
- known fingerprints
- handkerchief
- 3 glass microscope slides
- permanent marker
- tube of powdered graphite (from an art supply store)
- newspaper
- dust mask
- disposable safety gloves
- safety glasses
- small paper cup (2 oz)
- new makeup brush (from a pharmacy)
- ¾-inch transparent sticky tape in tape dispenser
- fingerprint card blank (Figure 3a)
- scissors
- magnifying glass (10–20X)
- access to a photocopier (optional)

What You Do:

1. Use a pen to label three blank 4 x 5-inch index cards with the following information in the top, left-hand corner:

EVIDENCE FINGERPRINT CARD

Date _____

Case No. _____

Fingerprint No. _____

Location: _____

2. Ask two friends' permission to allow you to fingerprint them. Use the direct fingerprinting procedure in Chapter 2 as a guide to making the two ten-print fingerprint sets (see page 27). These known fingerprints will be used later to identify the unknown latent print.

3. Using a handkerchief, wipe a glass microscope slide free of any stray fingerprints. Handle the slide only by the edges.

4. Close your eyes and have one of your friends (without telling you which friend) rub his or her finger against his or her nose or forehead (to collect skin oils) and place the finger in the center of the microscope slide. Have them use a permanent marking pen to label the slide "Q" for "questioned," or unknown. Make sure your friend remembers which finger and hand the print came from. Have your friend place the microscope slide in another room for you to analyze later.

5. Use the handkerchief to clean two more microscope slides of any stray fingerprints. Rub your right thumb against your nose or forehead and make a

single clear impression in the center of each slide. These two slides will be your "test" slides. Use a permanent marker to label them "T" for "test."

6. Now you will image and lift latent fingerprints from the smooth surface of the slides. Graphite powder will be your dusting powder. **Graphite is very slippery! Protect working surfaces with newspaper to collect any excess graphite. Do not inhale any graphite dust! Wear a dust mask, disposable safety gloves, and safety glasses whenever you work with graphite powder. Under adult supervision**, sprinkle a *small* amount of powdered graphite into a small paper cup, just enough to cover the bottom.

7. Dip a soft makeup brush into the cup and lightly dust the center area of one microscope slide containing your latent thumbprint (see Figures 6a and 6b). Lightly twirl the brush to apply a thin coating of graphite to the smooth surface.

8. As the print becomes visible, remove excess graphite powder by *lightly* and *gently* brushing it away. Try to lightly brush toward the direction of the ridgelines. Be careful not to destroy the print with too hard a brush stroke! This technique requires practice. Repeat this step on your other test latent thumbprint. Practice as many times as you need to until you are comfortable in being able to image a latent fingerprint.

FIGURE 6

Imaging and Lifting Latent Fingerprints

(a) Dip brush in graphite.

(b) Swirl brush onto print.

Remove print with clear tape:

(c)

(d)

(e)

(f) Place prints on evidence card.

9. To lift your thumbprint from the glass microscope slide, carefully grasp the *edge* of the transparent tape in its dispenser and pull it outward about five inches. Do not tear off the tape. Do NOT touch the bottom of the tape that has been unrolled. Position the untouched portion of the extended tape above the imaged fingerprint (see Figure 6c). Carefully smooth the tape over the developed print so that the fingerprint will stick to the tape (see Figure 6d).

10. Use a steady upward motion to gently pull the tape up off the fingertip (see Figure 6e). Carefully tear off the piece of tape from the dispenser.

11. Position the captured fingerprint over the center of a blank evidence fingerprint card. Carefully press the tape, containing the fingerprint, onto the paper. Trim any excess tape with scissors (see Figure 6f).

12. Use Steps 7 through 11 to dust, find, and recover your friend's fingerprint left on a glass microscope slide onto a blank evidence fingerprint card.

13. Use the analysis steps in Chapter 2 to analyze this recovered latent fingerprint, comparing it against the two ten-print reference fingerprint cards of your friends. Use a magnifying glass to help in your analysis. (If available, you may want to use a photocopier to enlarge the fingerprints for easier identification.) Can you get an identical match to a specific friend? A specific finger?

14. Practice! Have your friends handle or touch a variety of objects or surfaces. Use your newly

Tips For Developing Latent (Invisible) Fingerprints

Success in recovering (imaging) a latent fingerprint depends on the surface it is deposited on and the recovery technique used. There are two main types of surfaces—porous and nonporous. Porous surfaces, such as paper and wood, are able to absorb liquids. The surfaces are uneven and have openings, or pores. Nonporous surfaces, such as glass and tile, are solid, smooth, and sealed. They do not have pores. This chapter has examples of the following recovery techniques.

POROUS (paper, wood, cardboard, rubber)
- Visual (inspect with a 10–20X magnifying glass)
- Iodine fuming; see Case #8
- Ninhydrin; see Case #7

NONPOROUS (glass, tile)
- Visual (inspect with a 10–20X magnifying glass)
- Cyanoacrylate fuming; see Case #6
- Powder, graphite (black) / talcum (white); see Case #1

acquired skills as a forensic investigator to lift and identify latent fingerprints.

Science Project Ideas

- **DETERMINE HOW LATENT FINGERPRINTS ARE MADE.** Perspiration is known to play a central role in creating latent fingerprints. Test this factor by making latent fingerprints on a clean, smooth surface, free of any previous fingerprints, with (a) hands that have just been washed and carefully dried, (b) hands that have not been washed for awhile, (c) newly washed hands treated with a skin moisturizer, and (d) sweaty hands after vigorous exercise. Try lifting prints from each of these four classes of hands. Do these trials at least ten times. Use the same latent print-lifting technique to lift the prints from each test surface. Record your findings in your laboratory notebook. Can you readily lift a certain class of latent fingerprint? Do your results support this finding? Do oils (such as in skin moisturizers) have any effect? On a poster, illustrate your findings with photocopied enlargements of various lifted prints.

- **DETERMINE WHETHER LATENT FINGERPRINTS CHANGE OVER TIME.** Make a series of clear latent fingerprints on a clean, smooth surface, free of any fingerprints. Make a mark to identify the surface having the latent fingerprint. Place half of these surfaces with fingerprints on a windowsill that receives direct sunlight for several days, and half in a closet. Use the same technique to lift the prints from each test surface. Is there any difference in your ability to lift latent prints from an exposed or nonexposed surface? Try longer time periods, such as one week, two weeks, one month, or as long as you can. Based on your investigations, do latent fingerprints change with age? Does sunlight exposure improve or fade the prints over time? On a poster, illustrate your findings with photocopied enlargements of various lifted prints.

Chapter 5 has additional information that can help in your investigations.

CASE # 2

●●●●●●●●●●●●●●●●●

The Case of the Transferred Fingerprint

OBJECTIVE: To learn how to select falsified evidence.

THE SCOUNDREL: Trooper Edward Pilus (1950–   )

THE CRIME: EVIDENCE TAMPERING. On September 2, 1994, a Rockland County, New York, jury found state trooper Edward Pilus guilty of evidence tampering, giving false testimony, and official misconduct. Pilus was a sixteen-year veteran, and one of six New York State troopers who was the subject of a four-year fraud investigation. Ironically, Pilus had been one of forty investigators selected by the law enforcement organization to look for signs of evidence tampering—creating physical evidence outside of what is actually present at a crime scene.

At trooper Pilus's trial, special prosecutor Nelson E. Roth presented evidence to the court that Pilus actually planted evidence in a carjacking case. As the case investigator, Pilus was responsible for collecting fingerprint evidence. He followed the standard procedure with two latent fingerprints that he was able to recover from a broken glass window. He used a special clear sticky tape to lift the two visible fingerprints from the window of the stolen vehicle. Each of these lifted fingerprints was placed on an evidence card. The card was labeled to preserve the "chain of evidence" requirement—carefully documenting where and how the evidence was gathered, and by whom.

For some reason, he used the same clear sticky tape to lift a third fingerprint. However, this third fingerprint was not taken from the stolen vehicle, but from the booking card containing fingerprints of the suspect. What Pilus did not realize was that some paper fibers from the paper card were also transferred, along with the lifted fingerprint, to the evidence card.

In an unusual turn of events, this particular case went nowhere. The car's owner, a Virginia man, refused to testify against the suspect carjacker. Officially, this case was closed. But the tampered evidence remained in the case file to be discovered later by investigators who were reviewing all cases handled by Pilus from 1984 to 1992.

In Washington, an FBI forensic investigator peering through a microscope easily detected the stray paper fibers picked up by the sticky tape on the third print (see Figure 7). The presence of these fibers suggested that the print itself had been fraudulently transferred from the booking card and placed into evidence to insure a conviction.

At his trial, Mr. Roth stated that "Apparently, [Pilus] found it easier to fabricate evidence than to find it legitimately."

FIGURE 7

Paper Fibers

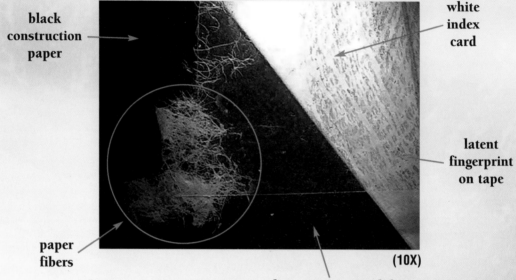

black construction paper

white index card

latent fingerprint on tape

paper fibers

(10X)

glass microscope slide

Paper fibers can be seen after a fingerprint was collected with clear sticky tape from a fingerprint card.

Today, the New York State Police have new procedures to prevent this type of evidence tampering. Any fingerprint match in a criminal case must be both photographed and confirmed by another investigator.

Five of the six troopers who were charged eventually pleaded guilty. All five are serving prison terms. The sixth was acquitted twice in a separate trial.

P R O J E C T :

Detecting Tampered Evidence

In this investigation, the crime scene centers around fingerprints removed from a broken front door window, and those lifted from a fingerprint reference card. See if your friends can determine which fingerprints were lifted from the window and which show evidence of tampering.

What You Need:

- **2 friends**
- **2 blank fingerprint file cards**
- **black ink pad (from office supply store)**
- **5 microscope slides**
- **piece of a newspaper (3 x 5 inches)**
- **piece of a magazine picture (3 x 5 inches)**
- **piece of red construction paper (3 x 5 inches)**
- **access to a sink for washing hands**
- **¾ -inch transparent sticky tape in tape dispenser**
- **permanent marker**
- **magnifying glass (10–20X)**
- **white, unlined index card**
- **desk lamp**
- **piece of black construction paper (3 x 5 inches)**

What You Do:

1. Carefully make a two ten-print fingerprint reference set of fingerprints of a friend using a blank fingerprint card (see Figure 3a) and a black ink pad. To make the inked direct print, begin with the small

finger of your friend's left hand. Carefully and gently take hold of it and roll it on top of the ink pad. Then move it to the correct position on the blank fingerprint card and roll it onto the card in a single, smooth motion. Repeat this process with each of the remaining nine fingers; left hand, then the right hand. Then repeat with a second set on a second fingerprint reference card.

2. Ask your friend to leave some of his or her fingerprints on some test surfaces. Your friend may have to re-ink the finger(s) to make sure that a dark, clear impression is made. Have your friend leave a single inked fingerprint on each of the following surfaces:

   ▪ glass microscope slide that will simulate a piece of window glass
   ▪ piece of newspaper
   ▪ piece of magazine picture
   ▪ piece of red construction paper

   Your friend should not tell you which finger or fingers were used to make the fingermarks (although he or she should record which finger was used for each print so you can confirm later).

3. Have your friend carefully wash away the ink from his or her fingers at a sink using soap and water.

4. Use the sticky tape lift technique for each of the black fingerprints from the five different surfaces (including one of the fingerprints from one of the

ten-print reference file cards). Use Figure 6 as a guide. Carefully apply the tape, press it down, and then lift each print from the surface.

5. As each of the five fingerprints are lifted, transfer and apply them to a separate glass microscope slide for examination. Use a permanent marker to label each slide as follows:

   - **Fingerprint #1**—lifted fingerprint from glass ("window")
   - **Fingerprint #2**—lifted fingerprint from newspaper
   - **Fingerprint #3**—lifted fingerprint from magazine picture
   - **Fingerprint #4**—lifted fingerprint from red construction paper
   - **Fingerprint #5**—lifted fingerprint from the fingerprint card

6. Have another friend act as the fingerprint examiner. His or her task is to carefully examine each of the five prepared fingerprints using a magnifying glass. Do not let the fingerprint examiner know exactly how the five fingerprints were obtained. Instead, the examiner should be told that it is important to confirm that each was lifted from a broken window. Also, the examiner's task will be to determine if all five lifted fingerprints are from the same individual.

7. In making the analysis, the examiner will need to study each fingerprint slide over a lighted light and dark surface. This will help show any unusual

features. The examiner should first place the fingerprint slide over a white, unlined index card. The fingerprint slide should be lit from above using a desk lamp and examined through a magnifying glass. After examining the fingerprint slide over a light background, the examiner should then place it over a piece of black construction paper. The examiner should also look closely at the areas around the actual fingerprint for anything out of place—stray fibers or other matter that should not be expected. The presence of any unusual artifacts should be recorded along with the details of Level I, II, or III criteria (see Chapter 2).

8. Each of the fingerprints on the five fingerprint slides should be compared to the fingerprints on the fingerprint card. Can any matches, with at least twelve points of similarity, be confirmed?

9. What are the fingerprint examiner's conclusions? Were all five fingerprints from the same individual? Were all five lifted from a broken window as reported? Were there any unusual circumstances associated with any of the lifted fingerprints? If so, how were they discovered?

See Chapter 5 for case analyses.

Science Project Idea

CAN YOU FIND A WAY NOT TO LEAVE FINGERPRINTS, WITHOUT USING GLOVES? There are commercial hand barrier cream products (such as DEB® Hand Barrier Cream, available at an auto parts store) that are applied by rubbing your hands together to create a "second skin" for protection against certain chemicals or processes. Can this "second skin" prevent transfer of a latent print to a smooth surface?

Obtain some of this product and apply it to your hands. Try touching a clean glass slide with your treated fingers. Then use the graphite fingerprint dusting technique (see Figure 6). Can you image a latent fingerprint? How effective are these barriers in providing "fingerprint protection" over time? On various surface types?

CASE # 3

The Case of the Telling Fingermark

OBJECTIVE: Examining fingerprint casts.

THE SCOUNDREL: Thomas Jennings (?–1912)

THE CRIME: BURGLARY AND MURDER. On September 19, 1910, it was a quiet night in Chicago. Clarence B. Hiller, his wife, and four children were asleep in their home. Late that night, Mrs. Hiller awoke and saw that the hall gaslight, normally on, was not lit. She shook

her husband awake and asked him to investigate. Clarence Hiller began a search of the house. As he went down the staircase, he met a prowler who was armed with a pistol. They struggled, both falling down the staircase. In the struggle, Hiller was shot twice. Hearing the shots and commotion, Mrs. Hiller screamed. The prowler fled, leaving Clarence Hiller dead of two gunshot wounds.

Police investigating the shooting determined that the point of entry into the house was the kitchen. The porch railing near the kitchen window had just been painted. As police examined the area around the kitchen, they noticed that the drying paint on the railing held the fresh imprint of four fingers. These paint impressions were preserved as evidence.

The police also searched the inside of the house. They looked into every room. In one of the children's rooms, they discovered sand on the floor. The sand appeared to be consistent with a sandy area in the backyard. They also recovered three shell cartridges at the foot of the stairway and two lead slugs in the stairway wall.

In the early morning of September 20, Thomas Jennings, a known burglar, was stopped by two police officers. The officers noticed that he was limping. Why was he out so late? After getting different answers to the same questions, the officers searched Jennings. On him, they found a loaded pistol. The police arrested Jennings.

In their investigation, police learned that Jennings had been paroled from prison in August of 1910 for a previous burglary conviction. Because of his imprisonment, Jennings had a fingerprint card on file. Police compared these known fingerprints with the four left-handed fingerprint impressions made in the paint on the house railing. All four prints matched.

At the Jennings trial, four fingerprint experts testified. Their expert testimony—though challenged by the defense—conclusively linked Thomas Jennings to the murder. It was the first case in the United States where fingerprint evidence alone was used to convict a felon.

Following an appeal, the supreme court of Illinois upheld Jennings's conviction. In *People* v. *Jennings* (1911) the court agreed that fingerprints were acceptable as evidence in a court of law.

The court ruled that "there is a scientific basis for the system of fingerprint identification, and that the courts are justified in admitting this class of evidence; that this method of identification is in such general and common use that the courts cannot refuse to take judicial cognizance of it."

On February 11, 1911, Jennings was found guilty. Five days later he was hanged.

PROJECT:

Can a Fake Finger Be Created?

Biometrics is the study of the physical characteristics that make us unique, and the ways to measure them. There are several biometric scanning identification systems for different portions of the body that are currently in use.

- **face**—the analysis of facial characteristics
- **fingerprint**—the analysis of fingerprint ridge patterns
- **retina**—the analysis of the capillary vessels located at the back of the eye
- **iris**—the analysis of the colored muscular ring that surrounds the eye's pupil

Many people believe that biometrics will play a role in future computers and electronic commerce. In the future, computers would include a fingerprint scanner. You would place your index finger on the scanner plate and have it scanned by a laser (see Figure 8a). The computer would analyze and compare the scanned ridge pattern to a digital image stored in its memory. If a match occurred, you would be allowed access to use credit card information to make electronic purchases.

Some of these devices, like the fingerprint scanner, have a major shortcoming—they cannot tell if they are scanning an actual body part. Latex rubber models and fingerprint patterns made on Gummi Bear candies can trick typical fingerprint scanners.

See if you can create an artificial fingerprint. Although you probably will not be able to test it on a fingerprint scanner, you will be able to see if your artificial finger can fool your friends!

What You Need:

- an adult
- direct fingerprint (Chapter 2) or lifted fingerprint (Case #1)
- magnifying glass (10–20X)
- access to a photocopier
- transparent acetate sheet
- cuticle scissors
- Elmer's® clear Squeez'n Caulk (from a home supply store)
- forceps (optional)
- handkerchief
- glass microscope slide
- tube of powdered graphite (from an art supply store)
- paper cup
- newspaper
- dust mask
- disposable safety gloves
- safety glasses
- clean makeup brush (from a pharmacy)
- ¾-inch transparent sticky tape in tape dispenser
- unlined index card
- scissors
- pen or pencil
- friends

What You Do:

Making an Artificial Finger

Use Figure 9 as a guide in making an artificial fingerprint.

FIGURE 8

Biometric Scanners

(a)

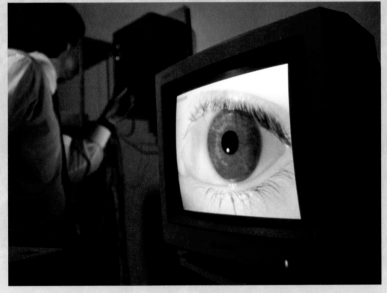

(b)

(a) A fingerprint scanner uses a laser to scan a fingerprint. The scan can then be compared to a fingerprint scan stored in the scanner.

(b) An iris scanner can work under the same idea; a person's iris is scanned and compared to a stored image.

1. Locate a direct index finger fingerprint that has well-developed ridgeline patterns. (Either make a new, known print on a card, as shown in Figure 4, or use one from your fingerprint card database.) Use a magnifying glass to confirm that there are no obvious faults with the fingerprint.

2. To make an artificial copy of an original fingerprint, you will need to make a mold. Obviously, the mold must be able to produce ridgeline patterns that are exactly like those of the original finger. No changes or distortions should occur.

   A simple, but effective, mold is to photocopy a fingerprint onto a transparent acetate sheet. In the photocopying process, the toner is fused to the acetate sheet in a raised pattern identical to a fingerprint pattern.

   Make a photocopy of the clear fingerprint onto a transparent acetate sheet (see Figure 9a).

3. Lay the photocopied acetate sheet on a table. Make sure that the fused toner surface is facing up.

4. Use cuticle scissors to cut off the tip of the caulk bottle at a slight angle. This will help in applying the material.

5. Carefully apply a thin layer of caulk over the entire photocopied fingerprint on the acetate sheet. Make sure that you apply the material so that there is at least a ¼ to ½-inch margin of material laid down around the fingerprint (see Figure 9b).

FIGURE 9
●●●●●●●●●●●●●●●

Making an Artificial Fingerprint

(a)

Fingerprint
on acetate

(b) 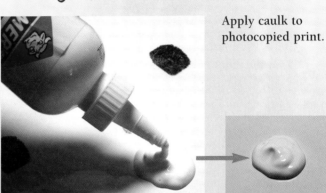 Apply caulk to
photocopied print.

(c)

Allow caulk to dry.

(d)

Lift the caulk from the print.

(e)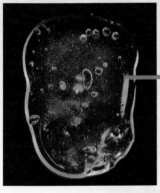

Examine ridgeline details, using a magnifying glass.

●●●●●●●●●●●●●●●

6. Allow the applied material to thoroughly dry for at least one week (see Figure 9c).

7. Use forceps, or your fingernail, to carefully lift up and separate the dried caulk from the acetate sheet all the way around the photocopied fingerprint (see Figure 9d).

8. Carefully, use your finger to gently pull on this exposed ring of material and pull the remainder of it away from the acetate sheet. Try not to stretch or distort the caulk material as you are lifting it from the acetate sheet.

9. Use a magnifying glass to examine the ridgeline surface. You should be able to observe clear, distinct fingerprint ridgeline detail (see Figure 9e).

Using an Artificial Finger to Make a Latent Fingerprint

Use Figure 10 as a guide to making a latent fingerprint with the artificial finger.

1. Use a handkerchief to clean a microscope slide of any stray fingerprints. Rub your finger against your nose or forehead. Then rub this finger onto the ridge surface of the artificial finger to transfer the collected skin oils (see Figure 10a). Press this ridge surface of the artificial finger into the center of the microscope slide to make a single clear impression (see Figure 10b).

FIGURE 10
●●●●●●●●●●●●●●●●●●

Making a Latent Fingerprint with an Artificial Finger

(a)

(b)

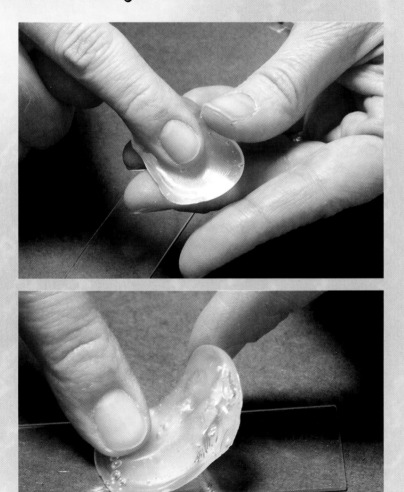

(a) Rub the ridged surface of the artificial print with skin oil.

(b) Press the ridged surface onto a microscope slide.

●●●●●●●●●●●●●●●●●●

2. **Under adult supervision**, sprinkle a small amount of powdered graphite into a small paper cup, just enough to cover the bottom. **Graphite is very slippery! Protect working surfaces with newspaper to collect any excess graphite. Do not inhale any graphite dust! Wear a dust mask, disposable safety gloves, and safety glasses whenever you work with graphite powder.**

3. Dip the cosmetic brush into the cup containing powdered graphite and lightly dust the center area of one microscope slide containing the artificial latent fingerprint.

4. After the print is imaged, remove excess graphite powder by lightly and gently brushing it away. As the fingerprint is exposed, brush toward the direction of the ridgeline pattern. Be careful not to destroy the print with too hard a brush stroke!

5. To lift the print from the glass microscope slide, carefully grasp the edge of the transparent tape in its dispenser and pull it outward about two inches. Do not tear off the tape. Do NOT touch the bottom of the tape that has been unrolled.

6. Position the untouched portion of the extended tape above the imaged artificial fingerprint. Carefully press the tape down onto the glass so that the graphite-imaged fingerprint will stick to the tape.

7. Use a steady upward motion to gently pull the tape up off the fingertip. Carefully tear off the piece of tape from the dispenser.

8. Position the captured fingerprint over the center of an unlined index card. Carefully press the tape, containing the fingerprint, onto the center of the index card. Trim any excess tape with scissors. Place a special mark on the index card so that only you know that its source is a molded artificial finger.

9. Use a magnifying glass to help you carefully compare the fingermark from the artificial finger to the original known index fingerprint.

   ▪ Is the orientation of the ridgelines in the artificial fingerprint the same as the known fingerprint?

   ▪ Are there signs of stretching or distortion?

   ▪ Can you find at least twelve points of similarity?

10. If the artificial fingerprint passes your inspection, ask some of your friends to inspect the two fingerprints. Are both fingerprints made by the same finger? What is their expert opinion?

11. See if you can "plant" this fake fingerprint for other investigators (your friends) to find and analyze.

Science Project Idea

WHAT IS THE BEST MOLD MATERIAL FOR CASTING FAKE FINGERPRINTS? The caulk material used in the above investigation was selected because it has strength, but great flexibility, for use as a stamp. Using fingerprints photocopied onto transparent acetate sheets, try to find other materials that can act as a fake finger. You may want to try these materials:

- Gummi Bear candy. Flatten the candy piece on a smooth surface to remove any marks. Carefully peel the candy away and press it onto the photocopied fingerprint. Remove the candy and use a magnifying glass to examine the pressed surface. Can ridgelines be seen? Try making a latent print impression on a clean microscope slide. Dust for the latent print impression. Transfer, and examine it. Are the qualities of the candy as good (or better) than the caulk material?
- Try other materials, such as Silly Putty, sticky tape, or clay.

The Case of Fingerprint #17

OBJECTIVE: Determining if fingerprints can lie.

THE SUSPECT: Brandon Mayfield (1967–   )

THE ACCUSATION: SUSPECTED INVOLVEMENT IN A TERRORIST BOMBING. On May 6, 2004, FBI agents arrested attorney Brandon Mayfield at his office in Portland, Oregon. They had an arrest warrant—a document signed by a judge authorizing the police to make an arrest. The warrant stated that Brandon Mayfield was a suspect in the March 11, 2004, bombing of four commuter trains in Madrid, Spain, that killed 191 people and injured over 2,000 others. The charge was based on a formal legal statement (an affidavit) prepared by a senior FBI fingerprint examiner, Terry Green. He had identified "in excess of 15 points of identification during his comparison" of Mayfield's known prints (from an earlier 1984 arrest) and an electronicly transmitted image of a print recovered and photographed from a plastic bag—fingerprint #17. The authorities found a plastic bag in a van near the train station from which the targeted trains had departed. The bag contained several explosive detonators.

The affidavit went on to describe how the match was made: Mayfield originally became a suspect when his print was identified as one of fifteen possible matches through FBI's Automated Fingerprint Identification System (AFIS). An FBI examiner then reviewed and confirmed that the Madrid print belonged to Mayfield. Two other FBI senior fingerprint examiners also verified the match.

After Mayfield's arrest, reporters were able to interview Mayfield's wife, Mona. She told them: "I think it's crazy. We haven't been outside the country for 10 years. They found only a part of one fingerprint. It could be anybody." Her words would soon ring true—it was someone else.

Back on March 13, the Spanish authorities had requested an analysis on latent fingerprints that had been collected during the bomb investigation. Originally, eight different low-resolution print images were given to the FBI. The FBI AFIS system could not get a match. The FBI asked for better (clearer) images. They needed the ridgeline detail to be more visible for a computer scan.

The next day, an e-mail arrived with higher resolution images. On March 15, the FBI fingerprint examiner entered the new data from fingerprint #17 into the AFIS computer. By March 19, Mayfield's matching print (one of five suspect candidates) had been reconfirmed by AFIS and verified by another expert fingerprint examiner. It was digit #7—Mayfield's right-hand index finger. The FBI unit chief contacted the Spanish authorities by phone and stated that they had a match. FBI policy required the unit chief to conduct an independent examination of the fingerprint prior to contacting Spanish authorities. No such review was made. On April 2, the FBI provided copies of Mayfield's fingerprints to the Spanish authorities.

On April 13, Spanish authorities had reviewed the FBI analysis and found it "inconclusive." They asked the FBI for further clarification. The FBI provided a detailed exhibit supporting their conclusions that the Mayfield print matched fingerprint #17 on the plastic bag.

On May 19, the Spanish National Police advised the FBI that it had identified fingerprint #17 on the plastic bag as belonging to an Algerian male with a police record and a Spanish residency permit.

On May 20, a federal judge in Portland ordered Mayfield's conditional release. He was free from custody three days later, and the warrant against him was dismissed. On May 31, a Spanish high court judge issued an international arrest warrant for the Algerian, Ouhnane Daoud, charging him with 190 counts of murder.

In January 2005, Robert B. Stacey, chief of the FBI's Quality Assurance and Training Unit issued a report based on its internal investigation. It was frank and honest. Among its findings were:

- Only seven matching points (Level II details) could be found for AFIS data plotting; not the twelve to fifteen usually required—or stated in the affidavit.

- The agency should have insisted on better images for orientation and analysis. However, the review committee stated that the quality of the submitted image was not a factor in the results.

- The error was a human failure and not a methodology or technology failure. The agency had NOT followed its own rules: analysis, comparison, evaluation, and verification, or ACE-V. It was the examiners' application of this methodology that failed.

- A policy with an expanded standard, rather than the current twelve-point Level II standard, needed to be made for quality assurance.

Use a magnifying glass to carefully study and compare both Mayfield's left index finger reference print (Figure 11a) and the recovered fingerprint from the plastic bag (Figure 11b). To help you compare the prints, make a photocopy of the digitally enhanced fingerprint #17 (Figure 11c) onto a clear acetate sheet. Then enlarge Figure 11a and 11b prints equally (at least 200 percent). Place the acetate sheet over the copy of Mayfield's known print. What do you think?

See Chapter 5 for a case analysis.

FIGURE 11

Madrid Bombing Case: Fingerprints

(a)

(b)

(c)

(a) Fingerprint of Brandon Mayfield's left index finger, from his arrest fingerprint card.

(b) Fingerprint #17 from a plastic bag near a Madrid railroad station.

(c) Digitally enhanced photo of fingerprint #17 to show ridgeline detail.

P R O J E C T :

Investigating Other Human Ridge Patterns

On May 12, 1999, an Illinois appellate court accepted, in *People* v. *Davis*, the testimony of Illinois State Police experts who considered that lip prints are unique like fingerprints and are a positive means of identification. See if you can confirm the state's findings by examining lip ridges.

What You Need:

- red lipstick
- white, unlined index cards
- magnifying glass (10–20X)
- some friends
- napkin

What You Do:

1. Apply a moderate amount of lipstick to your lips and carefully make a clear impression on a white index card. Make sure that your mouth is slightly open and that your lips are not pursed or pressed together.
2. Use a magnifying glass to scan the print. Can you discern consistent ridgeline patterns?
3. Make a lip ridge reference card by writing the following information on the upper top left-hand portion of an unlined index card.

Date: _____

Name: _____

Age: _____

4. Have your friends participate by offering to make lip ridge patterns for examination. Ask them to complete Step 1, and make a lip impression on a completed lip ridge reference card.

5. Use a magnifying glass to examine and compare various lip ridge patterns from various individuals. Are they all different?

6. Have one of your friends (whose reference lip print you have) leave a clear "unknown" lip print on a napkin. Can you make a positive identification? How many points of similarity can you find?

Chapter 5 has additional analysis information on lip ridge prints and their acceptance as a reliable method of identification.

Newborns are routinely foot printed as a means of ensuring unmistakable identity. If you can acquire a photocopy of your infant footprint, compare your big toe print (infant footprint) with your corresponding toeprint of today. Are the ridge patterns identical?

Science Project Idea

EXAMINING PHOTOCOPIES OF FINGERPRINTS. Fingerprint examiners are asked to make a comparison using a photocopied fingerprint instead of using the original. Sometimes these copies are many generations (a copy of a copy) old. Design an experiment that investigates how photocopying degrades ridgeline detail.

For example, make a copy of a direct fingerprint from one of your reference cards. Make a copy of this first copy. Make a copy of the second copy. Make a copy of the third copy. Examine the fourth-generation copy and compare it to the original reference fingerprint. Do you observe any changes in ridgeline detail?

Make a poster that presents your findings.

CASE # 5

The Case of the Yellow Patch

OBJECTIVE: Preventing art fraud by confirming an artist's identity.

THE ART RESTORER: RESTORATION OF *THE ADORATION OF THE CHRIST CHILD*. Leonardo da Vinci (1452–1519) recognized the value of fingerprints in identification. He is known to have left his fingermark—as a kind of signature—on various paintings and documents. One example is his masterpiece *Lady with an Ermine* hanging in the Czartoryski Museum, Cracow, Poland. Art historians (persons knowledgeable in the history of an artist and their work) use fingerprints—when they are left—as one means of proving that an artwork is genuine.

In early 2005, art historians had been given the chance to solve another mystery centered around Leonardo da Vinci. Is the painting *The Adoration of the Christ Child* by the great Renaissance master? Until now, most scholars say that it is the work of a friar (a member of a religious order, the Dominicans), Fra Bartolommeo (1472–1517).

The painting had just undergone a year-long cleaning and restoration by Elisabetta Zatti, an art

77

restorer. In a press conference she said: "It didn't exactly jump out at first. I wouldn't have found it if I hadn't been using my microscope. But when I had cleaned down to the original paint, I noticed a slightly yellow patch in the top left part of the sky, right near the edge. It's clearly a fingerprint left while the paint was still wet," said Zatti. "But we still don't really know whose finger it belongs to."

The artwork is awaiting a forensic fingerprint examiner's verdict.

PROJECT:

Investigating Three-Dimensional Fingertip Impressions

What You Need:

- clay
- friends
- reference fingerprints
- magnifying glass (10–20X)

What You Do:

1. Take two small pieces of modeling clay and roll them into balls.
2. Flatten the balls of clay on a smooth surface such as a desktop.
3. Carefully remove the clay "pancakes" and turn them upside down to reveal a smooth, shiny surface.

4. Have one of your friends (who you have reference fingerprints of) make a clear thumbprint impression in both smooth clay surfaces. Make sure you don't know which friend is making the fingermark. Have your friend make one clay impression using his or her left thumb, and the other using the right thumb.

5. Have one of your friends return these two clay pieces to you—without you knowing who made the thumbprints.

6. Use a magnifying glass to examine the fingerprint impressions. Study both carefully. Can you identify the individual who made them? The finger that made them?

   See Chapter 5 for a sample analysis.

Science Project Idea

EXAMINING FINGERPRINT IMPRESSIONS. You can make impressions of your fingerprint in a variety of different materials that will later harden, preserving them. Try clay, maple syrup, paint, and glue. Are all of these materials good preservers of fingerprint impressions? Use a magnifying glass to identify the fingerprint(s) in these sample materials. Compare the observed ridgeline detail to that of the identical fingerprint on a reference card. Is a particular material best at preserving ridgeline details?

C A S E # 6

• • • • • • • • • • • • • • •

The Case of the Soot-Covered Latent

OBJECTIVE: Exposing latent fingerprints on nonporous surfaces.

THE SCOUNDREL: Roy Warren (1952–   )

CRIME: ARSON. In March 1981, Houston, Texas, arson investigators (forensic experts who investigate the causes of a fire) were worried. They had a scorched gasoline container that was recovered from a burned-out apartment. They were hopeful that they could recover any latent fingerprints from the gas can—but fearful that the intense fire had destroyed any fingerprint evidence.

The gasoline can was sent to the Houston Arson Bureau. There, a talented and experienced forensic investigator, B. W. Emmons, went to work. He used sticky tape to lift the soot off the container and expose any fingerprints below. Emmons was patient. He carefully removed all the soot from the burned gasoline can. He spent hours at the task. At last, he was rewarded with a single fingerprint. The print matched that of Roy Warren, the victim's boyfriend. Warren had used gasoline to start a fire in his girlfriend's apartment after a quarrel with her. Presented with forensic evidence that linked him to the crime, he pled guilty. He was sentenced to eight years' probation.

When a local reporter asked Mr. Emmons how the fingerprint managed to escape the intense heat, he said he could not explain it. The reporter, after contacting the FBI, was told that soot coats and protects a fingerprint in a fire.

PROJECT:

Exposing Latent Fingerprints Using Superglue

Superglue and Crazy Glue are trademarks of a class of adhesives (substances used to stick objects together) that contain a chemical called cyanoacrylate. These types of adhesives are known as "instant adhesives" that bond nonporous materials that have tiny amounts of water in them. As such, cyanoacrylates are excellent bonders of skin! The fumes of cyanoacrylates are used in a chemical technique in forensic science to react with the moisture-containing fingerprints.

What You Need:

- an adult
- 4 x 4-inch square of aluminum foil
- scissors
- string
- duct tape
- pickle jar, with lid

- black objects (metal, plastic, or glass)
- handkerchief
- tube of Crazy Glue or Superglue (cyanoacrylate adhesive)
- access to a photocopier
- sheet of black construction paper (8½ x 11 inches)
- magnifying glass (10–20X)
- a friend

What You Do:

1. Make an aluminum foil "boat" by bending the edges of a 4 x 4-inch square of foil upward (see Figure 12a).

2. Use scissors to cut a 3-inch length of string.

3. Use a piece of duct tape to attach one end of the 3-inch piece of string to a pickle jar lid (see Figure 12b).

4. Attach a black-colored object to the other end of the string.

5. Wipe the black object clean of fingerprints using a handkerchief.

6. Make a single, clear fingerprint by rubbing a finger against your nose and carefully touching it to the middle of one side of the black object.

7. Place the aluminum foil "boat" in the bottom of the pickle jar.

WARNING! Be careful not to get any cyanoacrylate adhesive on your skin. The cyanoacrylate may affect the material you are testing.

FIGURE 12

Using Cyanoacrylate Fuming to Image Latent Fingerprints

(a)

aluminum foil "boat"

(b)

string

tape

black object

latent fingerprint

cyanoacrylate

(c)

(a) Prepare materials.

(b) Fuming apparatus setup.

(c) This photograph shows a latent fingerprint collected using this set-up.

8. **Have an adult** add 15–20 drops of cyanoacrylate adhesive to the center of the aluminum foil in the pickle jar.

9. Carefully lower the test object containing the latent fingerprint into the jar and screw the lid tightly.

10. Let the print develop for at least three hours. Since the chemical deposits left by the reaction are white, look for a white fingerprint image.

11. When the image has developed, carefully unscrew the lid and remove the object. Place it, developed fingerprint down, on the glass plate of a photocopier. Place a sheet of black construction paper on top of the object. Close the photocopier machine cover. Make photocopies of the exposed latent fingerprint for analysis.

12. Examine the recovered prints with a magnifying glass.

13. **Have an adult** dispose of the cyanoacrylate by rolling up the unused material in the aluminum foil and throwing it away.

14. Have a friend pick up and handle another black metal, plastic, or glass object. See if you can recover his fingerprint(s).

Science Project Idea

HOW EFFECTIVE ARE CYANOACRYLATE FUMES AT DEVELOPING LATENT FINGERPRINTS? Use the cyanoacrylate fuming process to image latent fingerprints on a variety of surfaces. Try comparing porous (paper, cardboard, wallpaper, rubber, leather, wood, and clothing) to nonporous (tile, metal, glossy side of a photograph, plastic bag, and glass). Make enlarged photocopies of your results. Prepare a poster that shows your techniques and results.

CASE #7

●●●●●●●●●●●●●●●●

The Case of Exhibit #62

OBJECTIVE: Exposing latent fingerprints on porous surfaces.

THE SCOUNDREL: Timothy J. McVeigh (1968–2001)

THE CRIME: MURDER AND CONSPIRACY. Federal authorities charged Timothy McVeigh with the April 19, 1995, bombing of the Federal Building in Oklahoma City, Oklahoma.

COURT TESTIMONY: Below is part of the official court record (transcript) from the McVeigh trial in Denver, Colorado. Here, Louis G. Hupp, an FBI latent fingerprint expert, is providing expert testimony in the case. He is being questioned by United States Attorney Patrick M. Ryan, and cross-examined by Mr. Stephen Jones, attorney for Timothy McVeigh.

Q. [Mr. Ryan] And then we talked about latent fingerprints. And that is what?

A. [Mr. Hupp] . . . a latent would be covered with something such as a thin film of perspiration or other foreign substance. And then when that touches a surface, these outlines are transferred, and they are generally invisible to the naked eye. The main separation in a latent print is a mere chance impression; an ink print is a purposeful reproduction.

Q. Now, before we start talking about those exhibits—let's remind the jury what you did with respect to Mr. Timothy McVeigh and his fingerprints before you obtained possession of Exhibit 62.

A. On the afternoon of April 21, 1995, I proceeded to Noble County in Oklahoma for the purpose of what we call major case printing [of] Mr. McVeigh, which included 10-roll impressions, as well as the entire friction ridge area of the palm.

Q. So you had a fingerprint card on Mr. McVeigh?

A. That is correct.

Q. And you examined the original [Exhibit 62] before coming here today, did you not?

A. That is correct.

Q. Tell us what this purports [what it is] to be, Exhibit 62 [see Figure 13].

A. This purports to be a Mid-Kansas Cooperative Association pink [sales] receipt. It carries a patron's account number that appears to be a 10 to me, dated 9-30-1994, and bearing the name Mike Havens [alias used by McVeigh's accomplice, Terry Nichols].

Q. All right. And what did Mr. Havens purchase on that date?

A. According to this, the quantity of 40/50, and the description was 34-0-0 [ammonium nitrate fertilizer]. And the price was at $5.40 each for a total price of $216.

Q. And it bears a—a receipt number of what?

A. M, as in Mary, 95504.

Q. All right. Now, what did you do in your laboratory at the FBI in Washington when you obtained possession of Exhibit 62 after you took it out of your safe?

A. After we took it out of our safe and, of course, we accounted for everything that was in the plastic bag and made notes to that effect, then it was my duty to process it for the presence of latent prints.

Q. All right. And did you do that?

A. Yes, I did.

Q. Tell the jury how you took latent prints from this document.

A. What I did was I processed it with ninhydrin. And developed two fingerprints.

Q. Do you have—did you bring with you today a blowup of the—of the latent fingerprint that you took from Exhibit 62, the—the Mid-Kansas receipt?

A. Yes, I did.

Q. And is that marked as Exhibit No. 63?

A. Yes.

Q. Would you identify what it is for the Court?

A. This is—this enlargement would be approximately a 12 times photographic enlargement of both the latent print and the ink print, and it would have red lines and numbers on it depicting the points of identity that I used to effect the identification.

FIGURE 13

CASE #5: Exhibit #62 McVeigh Trial

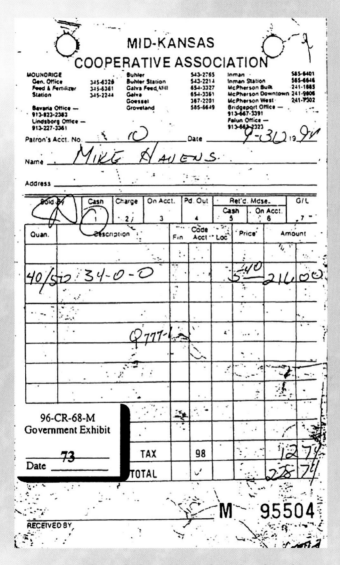

The first physical evidence linking McVeigh to bomb-making materials was a receipt for fertilizer.

Q. All right. And there are two prints on it, are there not?

A. That is correct.

Q. One print is what?

A. Is a known print of Mr. McVeigh, which I recorded.

Q. Okay.

A. And the other is the unknown print which I developed on this particular item.

Q. Now, if you will, Mr. Hupp, please turn to Exhibit 63. I would like for you to explain the comparison you made of the prints off the fert [fertilizer receipt]—excuse me—off of the Mid-America (sic) receipt and off of the—compared to the McVeigh fingerprint.

A. In effecting identification, it is my goal to find same or similar points of identity lying in the same relative position in two fingerprint impressions. . . . It is with these points that I have demonstrated to you, plus others that are illustrated in both the latents and the ink print, that caused me to form my opinion that the latent print that I developed on Government's Exhibit 62 was made by one and the same finger as the right index finger of the defendant, Mr. Timothy McVeigh.

Q. Do any two people have the same fingerprints?

A. No, sir.

Q. Now, Mr. Jones asked you some questions a moment ago with respect to when this fingerprint would have been placed on the receipt. I understand from what you told him that sometime between the date of this receipt and the time of the search of the Nichols' home is when Mr. McVeigh placed his fingerprint on this document.

A. That would be correct.

Q. And you don't know exactly when?

A. Have no idea.

This and other forensic testimony helped the government present an effective case to the jury. In June 1997, Timothy McVeigh was convicted in federal court on charges of murder and conspiracy in the April 19, 1995, bombing of the Federal Building in Oklahoma City, Oklahoma. He was executed by lethal injection on June 11, 2001, in Terre Haute, Indiana.

PROJECT:

Searching for Latent Fingerprints on Paper

Ninhydrin is a chemical that reacts with amino acids in sweat to give a dark purple color. It was proposed for fingerprint development in 1954. Ninhydrin has become the most widely used technique for fingerprint detection on paper surfaces. The treatment generally involves dipping the items in a ninhydrin solution and then leaving the prints to develop over 24 to 48 hours. Prints more than fifty years old have been developed by this process.

See if you can find and image a latent fingerprint, recover it, and identify its source.

What You Need:

- an adult
- safety glasses
- disposable safety gloves
- string (2 ft)
- clothespin
- access to a warm room
- tacks
- sales receipt
- a friend
- fingerprint ten-print file(s) (see Chapter 2)
- zip closure bag
- permanent marker
- ninhydrin solution (see Sources in Appendix)
- spray bottle
- forceps
- access to a photocopier
- magnifying glass (10–20X)

What You Do:

1. **With adult permission**, thread string through a clothespin in a warm room. Position a 2-foot length of string indoors using two tacks. The suspended clothespin will allow the treated paper to dry.

2. Obtain a sales receipt. Without your knowledge, have someone whose known fingerprints you already have on file (see Chapter 2) handle one of the receipts. To make sure that a clear print will be

made, have the handler rub his fingers on his nose or forehead before handling the sales receipt. Have this person place the receipt inside a zip closure bag. Have the person use a permanent marker to label the bag "Exhibit 1."

3. Have your friend provide you with the "evidence" without your knowing who touched the sales receipt.

4. **Have an adult** handle the ninhydrin solution. **CAUTION! Ninhydrin solution is flammable. Avoid all contact with open flames or heat sources. Have an adult** pour some ninhydrin solution into an empty spray bottle.

5. **Ask the adult** to carefully open the zip closure bag containing Exhibit 1 and use forceps to remove it from the bag.

6. **Have the adult** carry the sales receipt to the makeshift clothespin line. **Have the adult** use the suspended clothespin to grasp and hold the sales receipt.

7. **Have the adult** carefully spray both sides of the sales receipt with the ninhydrin solution. Allow the paper to dry overnight. The following day you should observe purplish marks on the paper, including your friend's fingerprint(s).

8. Make a photocopy of the chemically-treated fingerprint(s). Number each print if more than one is recovered.

9. Use a magnifying glass to examine and compare the photocopied chemically recovered fingerprint with known fingerprints. Can you determine which one of your friends handled the sales receipt?
See Chapter 5 for a sample analysis.

Science Project Idea

WHICH FINGERPRINT RECOVERY TECHNIQUE IS BETTER ON A WOOD SURFACE—DUSTING OR CHEMICAL DEVELOPMENT? Obtain two Popsicle sticks. Use a handkerchief to wipe both of them clean of any stray fingerprints. Have a known individual (one who you have a known set of fingerprints for) rub her nose or forehead with her right index finger and then apply her fingermark along both Popsicle sticks. Use the dusting latent print recovery method on one, and the chemical recovery method on the other Popsicle stick. Use a magnifying glass to examine recovered prints from each Popsicle stick. How effective is each method in recovering ridgeline detail? You may want to make enlarged photocopies to illustrate your findings.

The Case of the Tainted Confection

OBJECTIVE: Exposing latent fingerprints on porous surfaces.

THE SCOUNDREL: John Buettner-Janusch (1924–1992)

THE CRIME: POISONING. Dr. John Buettner-Janusch was a terribly bitter man. In 1980, Judge Charles L. Brieant, Jr., had sentenced him to five years in prison. He was convicted of making illegal drugs in his university laboratory. Out on parole, he wanted to even the score. He decided to use candy laced with two poisons— atropine and pilocarpine.

In February, 1987, Dr. Buettner-Janusch mailed two boxes of chocolate candy. One was sent to Judge Brieant, the other to a fellow professor at Duke University, Dr. J. Bolling Sullivan. Judge Brieant's wife was hospital- ized and Dr. Sullivan's wife and daughter became ill from eating the candy. The police were contacted.

Since the poisoned candy was sent through the mail, the FBI was brought into the case. The lab in Washington was able to quickly recover Dr. Buettner-Janusch's fingerprint from the candy box. Federal officers intercepted two more boxes of tainted candy sent to other professors. One contained a lethal dose of poison. Dr. Buettner-Janusch was arrested. He pleaded guilty to charges that he had mailed boxes of poisoned candy. He was sentenced to forty years in prison.

PROJECT:
Exposing Latent Fingerprints Using Iodine Vapors

Iodine fumes adhere to grease or oils on porous surfaces and appear as a yellow stain.

What You Need:
- an adult
- safety glasses
- disposable safety gloves
- scissors
- ruler
- sheet of white paper (2 x 2 inches)
- sticky tape
- baby food jar, with lid
- iodine crystals (science teacher)
- tweezers
- magnifying glass (10–20X)
- a friend
- printed receipt

96

What You Do:

SAFETY: Put on disposable safety gloves and safety glasses.

1. Cut a sheet of white paper to a 2 x 2-inch square. Do not touch the 2-inch-square section of the sheet with your bare fingers.

2. Carefully apply about a one-inch-long piece of sticky tape to the paper and attach it to the lid of a baby food jar.

3. Remove one plastic glove. Rub your nose with your index finger. Make a single finger impression in the center of the 2-inch-square piece of paper (see Figure 14a). Put the glove back on.

WARNING! Iodine is irritating to skin and eyes. Do not breathe vapors. Have an adult handle the iodine crystals.

4. **Have an adult, wearing disposable safety gloves**, add about ten iodine crystals to the bottom of the baby food jar.

5. Carefully lower the piece of paper containing the latent fingerprint into the jar and screw the lid tightly.

6. Let the print develop for three to five minutes, or until the print is visible. It will be yellow (see Figure 14b).

7. Open the jar. Use tweezers to remove the paper sample.

8. Close and reseal the jar.

FIGURE 14

Using Iodine to Image Latent Fingerprints

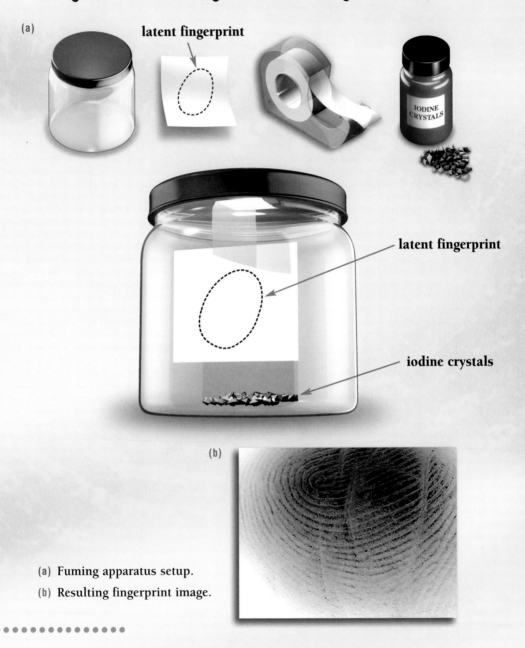

(a)

latent fingerprint

IODINE CRYSTALS

latent fingerprint

iodine crystals

(b)

(a) Fuming apparatus setup.

(b) Resulting fingerprint image.

9. Examine the paper with a magnifying glass. The developed print may disappear, as its iodine coating continues to evaporate.

10. **Have an adult** dispose of the unused iodine crystals.

11. Have a friend handle a printed receipt. Use the iodine fuming method to see if you can recover and identify his or her fingerprint(s).

Science Project Idea

HOW EFFECTIVE ARE IODINE FUMES IN DEVELOPING LATENT FINGERPRINTS? Use the iodine fuming process to image latent fingerprints on a variety of surfaces. Try comparing porous (paper, cardboard, wallpaper, rubber, leather, wood, and clothing) to nonporous (tile, metal, glossy side of a photograph, plastic bag, and glass). Make enlarged photocopies of your results. Prepare a poster that shows your techniques and results.

CHAPTER 4

●●●●●●●●●●●●●●●●●●●●●

Investigating the Crime

This chapter introduces a "crime" that you and your friends can solve using the information and cases presented in Chapters 2 and 3. This "crime" is based on an actual case. It is your responsibility to evaluate the presented evidence, reach conclusions, and provide findings of fact in a report to the director of the forensics laboratory.

THE PROFILE:

The Case of the Jumbled Thumbprint

In this fictional case, the River Vale, New Jersey, police have arrested a suspect in a drug case. When the suspect was fingerprinted, the desk sergeant noticed something very unusual—his fingertips had slices in them. The suspect told police that he had sliced his left thumb fingertip into small pieces and transplanted them onto his right thumb. He said "My fingertips have healed. I have new thumbprints. There is no way you can link me to my previous crimes."

Is there? The police have recovered an excellent latent thumbprint from an unsolved Westwood, New Jersey, jewelry heist in 1998. This print and his two

100

booking thumbprints are provided for your analysis. Can a match be made between any of the direct, unaltered thumbprints from a previous booking card and the latent thumbprint found at the crime? The head of the Bergen County forensic lab is confident that you can provide an ACE-V analysis and complete a report.

What You Need:
- **Figure 15**
- **access to a photocopier**
- **magnifying glass (10–20X)**
- **red-ink pen**
- **scissors**
- **glue stick**

What You Do:

Analysis Steps

1. **Have an adult** help you adjust a photocopier so that it will greatly enlarge the fingerprints in Figure 15.

2. Make two photocopies of the known left and right thumbprints (Figures 15a and 15b). Make two equal magnification enlargements of the recovered latent thumbprint (Figure 15c). Save one of each photocopy to help prepare an illustration for your report (see Step 7). Use the other for analysis.

3. Using a magnifying glass, carefully look over the enlarged photocopy of the known right and left booking thumbprints from the booking fingerprint card. Then look at the recovered print (15c). Do you

FIGURE 15

● ● ● ● ● ● ● ● ● ● ● ● ● ● ● ● ● ●

Thumbprints for the Case of the Jumbled Thumbprint

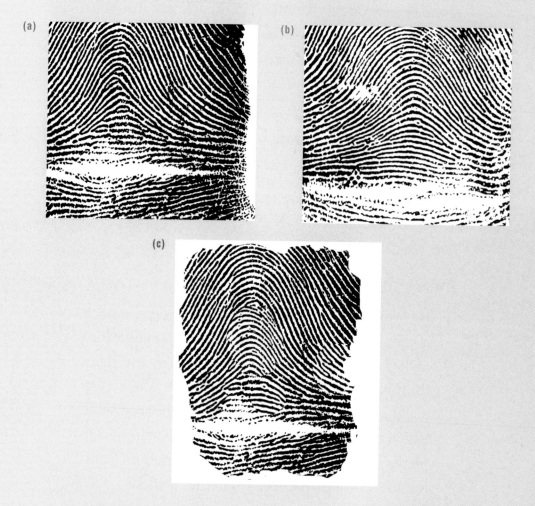

(a) Suspect's known unaltered left thumbprint from the booking fingerprint card.

(b) Suspect's known unaltered right thumbprint from the booking fingerprint card.

(c) Recovered latent thumbprint from New Jersey jewelry store.

● ● ● ● ● ● ● ● ● ● ● ● ● ● ● ● ●

see areas on the recovered fingerprint that show disrupted, unusual ridgeline patterns (e.g., altered, upside down, or misaligned)? Use a red pen to circle these unusual areas.

4. Using a magnifying glass, carefully look over the photocopy enlargements of both known thumb-prints. Can any discovered unusual ridgeline details in print 15c be matched to either of the known prints?

5. If you spot a possible match, circle the area in red ink on the photocopy. Draw a line connecting the two circled areas. Has there been an alteration of the recovered print (15c)?

6. Repeat Steps 4 and 5 with any other unusual ridgeline patterns.

7. Can you
   - identify Level I detail in each of the thumb-prints—known and latent?
   - identify any key features at Level II, and (if possible) Level III on either of the known thumbprints that can be used for identification purposes in the latent thumbprint?
   - identify a match between the latent thumbprint and any areas of the known thumbprints?

Assemble Your Findings

8. Use the other photocopies of the direct and latent prints to show how the recovered print (15c) was

altered. Can you show that the recovered print matches either of the known prints? You will need this diagram for your pretrial report.

Complete Your Report

9. Your findings are important to the successful prosecution of the case. The lab director requests that the report contain the following:
   - method(s) used in analysis
   - findings:
     - Level I findings
     - Level II findings
     - Level III findings (if possible)
   - a comparison diagram that summarizes your findings.

   Compare your findings to those in the analysis section (Chapter 5) of this book.

Case Analyses

This chapter contains analysis findings for many of the projects presented in this book.

CHAPTER 2

PROJECT: Practicing Fingerprint Ridge Identification Skills

The practice fingerprint in Figure 2 is a radial loop pattern. Figure 16 shows various identified ridge details of the practice fingerprint. Fingerprint ridge details are listed in their order of frequency—most to least frequent in occurrence: ending ridge, fork, short ridge, dot, bridge, hook, eye, double fork, delta, and triple fork.

FIGURE 16

Sample Analysis of Thumbprint

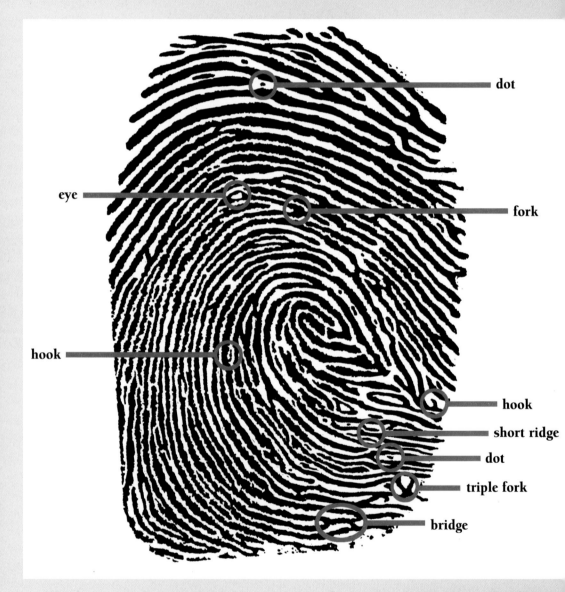

This fingerprint shows a radial loop pattern. Some fingerprint ridge details are identified.

PROJECT: Practicing Your Fingerprint Analysis Skills

1. All three fingerprints are ulnar loops.
2. Fingerprints #1 and #3 are direct matches, with twelve points of similarity (see Figure 17).
3. From the group of people you fingerprinted, you may have discovered that the loop is the most common fingerprint pattern. The percent occurrence is listed below for the general population:

60–65%	loop
30–35%	whorl
5%	arch

To calculate percent occurrence data for your investigation, take the number of occurrences of a particular fingerprint pattern and divide it by the total number of fingerprints taken. Multiply this number by 100 to get the percent occurrence. For example, say you had 4 arch fingerprint patterns out of 100 fingerprints. The percent occurrence would be:

$$4/100 = 0.04$$
$$0.04 \times 100 = 4 \text{ percent}$$

Also, the following general observations can be made: Individuals of African ancestry tend to have plenty of arches; individuals of European background tend to have frequent loops; and individuals of Asian ancestry tend to have a high frequency of whorls.

FIGURE 17

Analysis of Fingerprint Patterns and Points of Similarity

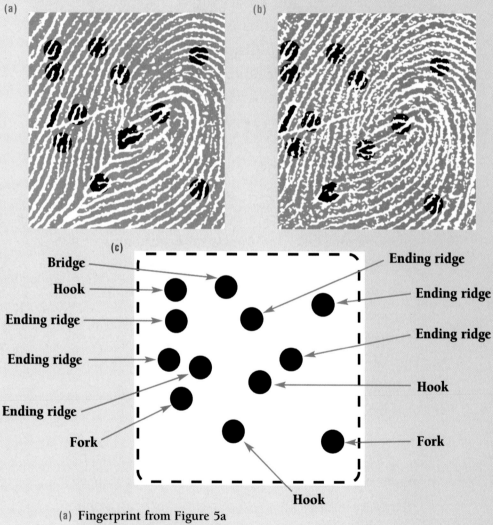

(a) Fingerprint from Figure 5a

(b) Fingerprint from Figure 5c

(c) There are twelve points of similarity between fingerprints (a) and (b).

- Can an individual have more than one general type fingerprint? *Yes.*
- Do identical twins have the same fingerprint type; on each finger? *No.*

● ● ● ● ● ● ● ● ● ● ● ● ● ● ● ● ● ●

CHAPTER 3

● ● ● ● ● ● ● ● ● ● ● ● ●

CASE #1. **The Case of the Solitary Fingerprint**

Science Project Ideas:

- **DETERMINE JUST HOW LATENT FINGERPRINTS ARE MADE.**

"Clean" fingertips will leave poor latent prints as compared to fingertips that have skin oils and perspiration. "Dirty" hands that have fingertips with particles of soil already clinging to finger ridges and soaking up skin oils and perspiration will leave relatively poor fingerprints.

When fingers come into contact with any relatively smooth surface, the friction of this contact will leave a ridge pattern. When powder is applied to the surface, it sticks to the deposited oil and perspiration to reveal a ridgeline pattern. Dusting is ideal on wood, metal, glass, plastics, Formica, and tile. It is less than ideal on paper, cardboard, and leather. Powders vary in color, stickiness, and photographic and magnetic qualities. The most common powder colors are black, white, gray, aluminum, red, and gold. The best color to use is one in sharp contrast to the surface color. For example, a white or gray powder works best on a dark surface, and a black powder works best on a lighter surface.

• **DETERMINE WHETHER LATENT FINGERPRINTS CHANGE OVER TIME.**

Based on recent studies by the Department of Energy on the chemical components of perspiration, a fingerprint image becomes "hardened" over time. Within weeks of its creation, it loses almost 85 percent of its weight—mostly water. The remaining chemical components (mostly fatty acids) chemically change into a harder, crystalline form. After sixty days, significant degrading of a fingerprint can occur.

But not all old fingerprints are beyond imaging—many chemical methods can image prints over half a century old!

• • • • • • • • • • • • • • • • •

CASE #2. The Case of the Transferred Fingerprint

In this example analysis, the submitted fingerprint evidence is examined using various light and dark backgrounds that allow the examiner to more easily detect any unusual artifacts such as fibers or other particles. Since the examiner was told to review the lifted fingerprints and confirm that they were lifted from a glass surface, the presence of paper fibers would not be expected.

Figure 18 shows an example of evidence tampering. Print (a) has been lifted from glass. Prints (b) through (e) reveal paper fiber evidence not expected for a latent print lifted from a glass surface. These prints have been lifted from various paper (e.g. porous) surfaces. In each case paper fibers can be observed (arrows, or within the circle), depending on the background used.

●●●●●●●●●●●●●●●●●●

CASE #4. **The Case of Fingerprint #17**

In a May 24, 2004, press release, the FBI stated:

> Upon review it was determined that the FBI identification was based on an image of substandard quality, which was particularly problematic because of the remarkable number of points of similarity between Mr. Mayfield's prints and the print details in the images submitted to the FBI.

Shortly after this public statement, the internationally recognized fingerprint examiner Allan Bayle gave an opinion on fingerprint #17: " . . . the clarity is good, and they are so dissimilar from Mayfield's that they should not have been declared a match by a competent examiner."

Note the large number of points of similarity and points of dissimilarity between Mayfield's known print and the recovered latent print in Figure 19.

FIGURE 18

Analysis of Examining Lifted Fingerprints for Evidence Tampering

This is an example analysis of five fingerprints submitted as being lifted from a window at a crime scene. Each fingerprint is at 10X magnification.

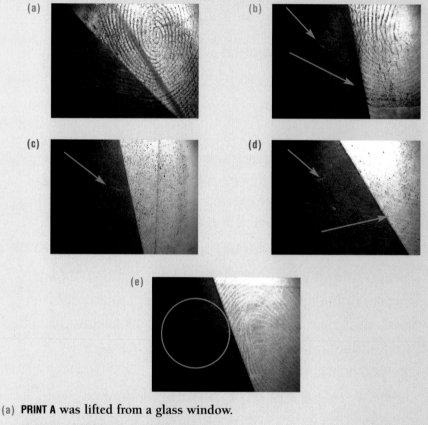

(a) **PRINT A** was lifted from a glass window.

(b) **PRINT B** was lifted from a newspaper.

(c) **PRINT C** was lifted from a magazine picture.

(d) **PRINT D** was lifted from red construction paper.

(e) **PRINT E** was lifted from a fingerprint card.

FIGURE 19
• • • • • • • • • • • • • • • •

Analysis—Brandon Mayfield Case

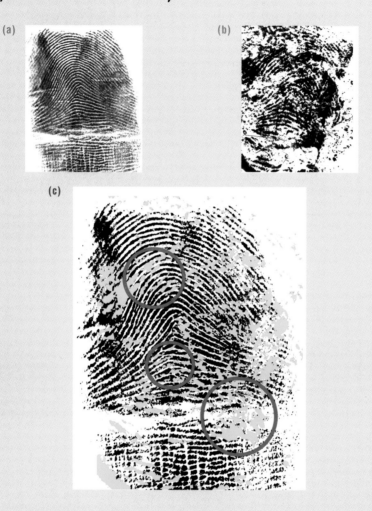

(a) Brandon Mayfield's left index finger fingerprint from his arrest fingerprint card.

(b) A copy of the latent fingerprint.

(c) When images a and b were digitally enhanced and combined, points of similarity (in red circles) and points of dissimilarity (in blue circle) were noted. The large number of points of dissimilarity pointed to Mayfield's innocence.

PROJECT: Investigating Other Human Ridge Patterns

See Figure 20. In *People* v. *Davis*, the Illinois Appellate Court accepted that:

- lip print identification is a "means of positive identification"
- it is "accepted by forensic science as a means of scientific comparison"
- the F.B.I. and the Illinois State Police "consider that lip prints are unique like fingerprints and are a positive means of identification"
- at least thirteen points of similarity between a standard and the partially blurred questioned print existed

• • • • • • • • • • • • • • • • • •

CASE #5. The Case of the Yellow Patch

PROJECT: Investigating Three-Dimensional Fingertip Impressions

Figure 21a shows a three-dimensional fingerprint impression in clay. Figure 21b shows the same fingerprint on paper. Four of the many matches are circled in corresponding colors.

FIGURE 20
●●●●●●●●●●●●●●

Analysis—Lip Ridges

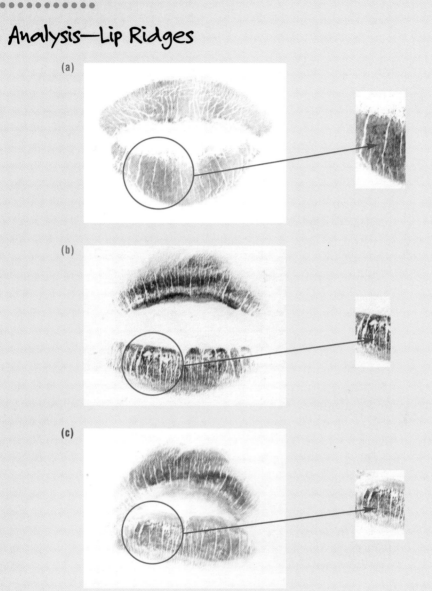

Lip prints are shown for (a) individual #1, (b) individual #2, and (c) individual #3. Lip prints b and c are from the same individual.

●●●●●●●●●●●●●●

FIGURE 21

Analysis—Investigating Three-Dimensional Fingertip Impressions

(a)

(b)

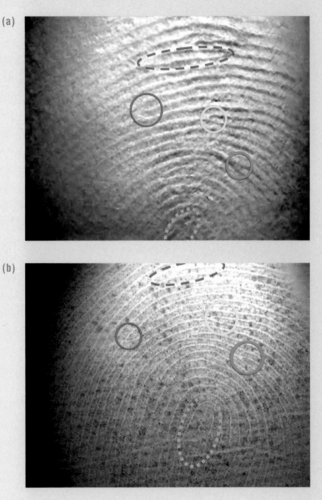

(a) Three-dimensional fingermark impression

(b) Known fingerprint

Points of similarity are circled in corresponding colors.

CASE #7. **The Case of Exhibit #62**

PROJECT: **Searching for Latent Fingerprints
on Paper**

Figure 22 shows known fingerprints from a friend (a–c) and a developed print from a receipt (d). The analysis in Figure 22e shows twelve similar points between the purple (developed) print and a friend's fingerprint. Twelve points of similarity equal a match.

● ● ● ● ● ● ● ● ● ● ● ● ● ● ● ● ● ● ● ●

CHAPTER 4
The Case of the Jumbled Thumbprint

- Both known thumbprints (Figures 23a and b) have a simple arch pattern. The recovered print (Figure 23c) has a simple arch pattern.
- The majority of the ridgeline patterns in the recovered print match the known right thumbprint (see the points of similarity in Figures 23b and c).
- The recovered print has been physically altered. Four areas were transferred from the left thumb (23a) to the right thumb (see colored areas in 23c).

In conclusion, the recovered print has ridgelines that match the right print (23b) and areas of transfer from the left thumb (23a). This places the suspect at the jewelry store.

FIGURE 22

Analysis—Chemically Developed Latent Prints

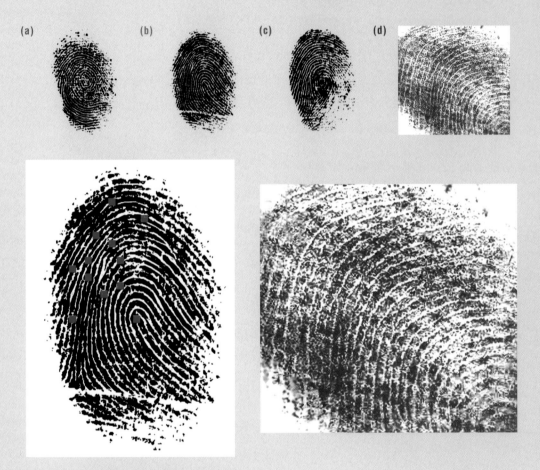

(a) Friend's right index finger.

(b) Friend's right middle finger.

(c) Friend's right ring finger.

(d) Chemically developed latent print (ninhydrin) from a receipt.

(e) An enlarged middle finger print and an enlarged ninhydrin print show twelve points of similarity; circles and squares indicate these matches.

FIGURE 23

●●●●●●●●●●●●●●

Analysis—Reconstructed Thumbprint

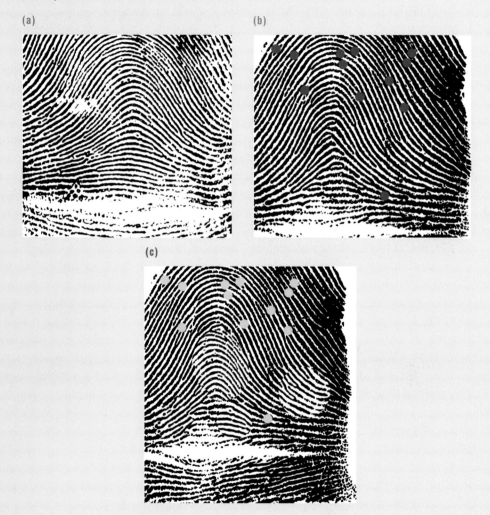

(a) Known left thumbprint from suspect.

(b) Known right thumbprint from suspect.

(c) Recovered print from jewelry store. The areas of surgical transfer are outlined in separate colors. Matching areas in figures (b) and (c) correspond to the dots.

●●●●●●●●●●●●●●

GLOSSARY

accomplice—A person who helps another commit a crime.

cyanoacrylate—A material used in a chemical method of developing latent fingerprints in which its vapors react with moisture in the fingerprint, turning it white.

direct print—A fingerprint impression made from a known source that serves as the reference standard.

elimination print(s)—Prints taken by investigators of individuals known not to be involved at the crime scene but whose fingerprints are known to be present. Their purpose is to eliminate unnecessary physical evidence.

evidence—Testimony, documents, and material objects presented at a trial to prove the existence or nonexistence of a fact.

findings—Legal conclusions acceptable by the court.

fingermark—Visible fingertip feature.

fingerprints—The unique patterns created by skin ridges found on the palm sides of fingers and thumbs.

forensic science—Field of science used in the judicial process.

fraud—Intent to deceive.

inconclusive—Leading to no conclusion or definite result.

iodine—Chemical used to develop latent fingerprints.

latent fingerprint—A fingerprint mark that is not visible, requiring chemical or physical treatment to make it visible.

ninhydrin—A chemical used to detect ammonia and amino acids, the building blocks of proteins. It reacts with these chemicals to form a deep blue or purple color. Ninhydrin is most commonly used to detect amino acids left in perspiration on fingerprints.

perpetrator—Individual who carries out a crime.

physical evidence—Material objects that prove the existence of a fact.

points of similarity—The number of identical matches of a particular ridge detail in a fingerprint of the same type.

porous—Able to absorb liquids.

pretrial report—A summary of the facts of a case including conclusions based on analysis.

testimony—Evidence given by a knowledgeable witness, under oath, as compared to evidence from writings and other sources.

APPENDIX
Science Supply Companies

Most of the materials required for investigations in this book are available at local stores. Items such as phenolphthalein solution and luminol can be obtained from the sources below. Most companies can be contacted on the Internet; some have online catalogs that make direct ordering easy.

1 **Aldon Corporation**
   Ninhydrin reagent; iodine
   221 Rochester Street
   Avon, NY 14414-9409
   800-724-9877
   http://www.aldon-chem.com

2 **Carolina Biological Supply Company**
   Ninhydrin reagent; iodine; microscopes
   2700 York Road
   Burlington, NC 27215
   800-334-5551
   http://www.carolina.com

3 **Flinn Scientific**
   Ninhydrin reagent; iodine; microscopes
   P.O. Box 219
   Batavia, IL 60510-0219
   800-452-1261
   http://www.flinnsci.com

4 **Frey Scientific**
   Ninhydrin reagent; iodine; microscopes
   P.O. Box 8101
   100 Paragon Parkway
   Mansfield, OH 44903
   800-225-3739
   http://www.freyscientific.com

5 **Neo/SCI**
   Inkless fingerprint cards; microscopes
   100 Aviation Avenue
   Rochester, NY 14624
   800-526-6689
   http://www.neosci.com

FURTHER READING

BOOKS

Camenson, Blythe. *Opportunities in Forensic Science Careers.* Chicago: VGM Career Books, 2001.

Conklin, Barbara Gardner, Robert Gardner, and Dennis Shortelle. *Encyclopedia of Forensic Science: A Compendium of Detective Fact and Fiction.* Westport, Conn.: Oryx Press, 2002.

Fridell, Ron. *DNA Fingerprinting: The Ultimate Identity.* New York: Franklin Watts, 2001.

———. *Solving Crimes: Pioneers of Forensic Science.* New York: Franklin Watts, 2000.

Morgan, Marilyn. *Careers in Criminology.* New York: McGraw-Hill, 2000.

Owen, David. *Police Lab: How Forensic Science Tracks Down and Convicts Criminals.* Buffalo, N.Y.: Firefly Books Ltd., 2002.

Platt, Richard. *Crime Scene: The Ultimate Guide to Forensic Science.* London: Dorling Kindersley, Ltd., 2003.

Rainis, Kenneth G. *Crime-Solving Science Projects: Forensic Science Experiments.* Berkeley Heights, N.J.: Enslow Publishers, Inc., 2000.

———. *Microscope Science Projects and Experiments: Magnifying the Hidden World.* Berkeley Heights, N.J.: Enslow Publishers, Inc., 2003.

Ramsland, Katherine. *The Forensic Science of C.S.I.* San Francisco: Berkley Publishing Group, 2001.

INTERNET ADDRESSES

CourtTV.com. Forensics in the Classroom. © 2002.
<http://www.courttv.com/forensics_curriculum>

Federal Bureau of Investigation. FBI Youth.
<http://www.fbi.gov/kids/6th12th/6th12th.htm>

INDEX

ABOUT THE AUTHOR

Kenneth G. Rainis is a microbiologist, illustrator, and microscopist, as well as a cofounder of Neo/Sci Corporation, a science education company in New York. He has a B.S. in biology and an M.S. in protozoology. He has authored numerous science labs and science project books. Mr. Rainis is also a contributor, reviewer, and safety consultant for a number of high school and college biology textbooks. He lives in New York with his wife and children.